THE SYRIAN
REBELLION

HERBERT AND JANE DWIGHT WORKING GROUP
ON ISLAMISM AND THE INTERNATIONAL ORDER

*Many of the writings associated with this
Working Group will be published by the Hoover Institution.
Materials published to date, or in production, are listed below.*

ESSAYS

Saudi Arabia and the New Strategic Landscape
Joshua Teitelbaum

Islamism and the Future of the Christians of the Middle East
Habib C. Malik

Syria through Jihadist Eyes: A Perfect Enemy
Nibras Kazimi

The Ideological Struggle for Pakistan
Ziad Haider

BOOKS

Freedom or Terror: Europe Faces Jihad
Russell A. Berman

The Myth of the Great Satan: A New Look at America's Relations with Iran
Abbas Milani

Torn Country: Turkey between Secularism and Islamism
Zeyno Baran

Islamic Extremism and the War of Ideas: Lessons from Indonesia
John Hughes

The End of Modern History in the Middle East
Bernard Lewis

The Wave: Man, God, and the Ballot Box in the Middle East
Reuel Marc Gerecht

Trial of a Thousand Years: World Order and Islamism
Charles Hill

Jihad in the Arabian Sea
Camille Pecastaing

The Syrian Rebellion
Fouad Ajami

HERBERT AND JANE DWIGHT WORKING GROUP ON ISLAMISM AND THE INTERNATIONAL ORDER

THE SYRIAN REBELLION

Fouad Ajami

HOOVER INSTITUTION PRESS
STANFORD UNIVERSITY | STANFORD, CALIFORNIA

www.hoover.org

Hoover Institution Press Publication No. 624

Hoover Institution at Leland Stanford Junior University, Stanford, California 94305-6010

First printing 2012
19 18 17 16 15 14 13 12   9 8 7 6 5 4 3 2

Manufactured in the United States of America

The paper used in this publication meets the minimum Requirements of the American National Standard for Information Sciences—Permanence of Paper for Printed Library Materials, ANSI/NISO Z39.48-1992. ♾

Cataloging-in-Publication Data is available from the Library of Congress.
ISBN 978-0-8179-1504-9 (cloth : alk. paper)
ISBN 978-0-8179-1506-3 (e-book)

*The Hoover Institution gratefully acknowledges
the following individuals and foundations
for their significant support of the*

**HOOVER
INSTITUTION
STANFORD
UNIVERSITY**

HERBERT AND JANE DWIGHT WORKING GROUP
ON ISLAMISM AND THE INTERNATIONAL ORDER:

Herbert and Jane Dwight

Beall Family Foundation

Stephen Bechtel Foundation

Lynde and Harry Bradley Foundation

Mr. and Mrs. Clayton W. Frye Jr.

Lakeside Foundation

The Hoover Institution gratefully acknowledges

PRESTON AND CAROLYN BUTCHER

for their significant support of this publication

For Leila, who arrived in the Spring

CONTENTS

F OR DECADES, THE THEMES of the Hoover Institution have revolved around the broad concerns of political, economic, and individual freedom. The Cold War, which engaged and challenged our nation during the twentieth century, guided a good deal of Hoover's work, including its archival accumulation and research studies. The steady output of work on the communist world offers durable testimonies to that time, and struggle. But there is no repose from history's exertions, and no sooner had communism left the stage of history than a huge challenge arose in the broad lands of the Islamic world. A brief respite, and a meandering road, led from the fall of the Berlin Wall on November 9, 1989, to the attacks upon the United States on September 11, 2001. Hoover's newly launched project, the Herbert and Jane Dwight Working Group on Islamism and the International Order, is our contribution to a deeper understanding of the struggle in the Islamic world between order and its nemesis, between Muslims keen to protect the rule of reason and the gains of modernity, and those determined to deny the Islamic world its place in the modern international order of states. The United States is deeply engaged, and dangerously exposed, in the Islamic world, and we see our working group as part and parcel of the ongoing confrontation with the radical Islamists who have declared war on the states in their midst, on American power and interests, and on the very order of the international state system.

The Islamists are doubtless a minority in the world of Islam. But they are a determined breed. Their world is the Islamic emirate, led by self-styled "emirs and mujahedeen in the path of God" and legitimized by the pursuit of the caliphate that collapsed with the end of the Ottoman Empire in 1924. These masters of terror and their foot soldiers have made it increasingly difficult to integrate the world of Islam into modernity. In the best of worlds, the entry of Muslims into modern culture and economics would have presented difficulties of no small consequence: the strictures on women, the legacy of humiliation and self-pity, the outdated educational systems, and an explosive demography that is forever at war with social and economic gains. But the borders these warriors of the faith have erected between Islam and "the other" are particularly forbidding. The lands of Islam were the lands of a crossroads civilization, trading routes, and mixed populations. The Islamists have waged war, and a brutally effective one it has to be conceded, against that civilizational inheritance. The leap into the modern world economy as attained by China and India in recent years will be virtually impossible in a culture that feeds off belligerent self-pity, and endlessly calls for wars of faith.

The war of ideas with radical Islamism is inescapably central to this Hoover endeavor. The strategic context of this clash, the landscape of that greater Middle East, is the other pillar. We face three layers of danger in the heartland of the Islamic world: states that have succumbed to the sway of terrorists in which state authority no longer exists (Afghanistan, Somalia, and Yemen); dictatorial regimes that suppress their people at home and pursue deadly weapons of mass destruction and adventurism abroad (Iraq under Saddam Hussein, the Iranian theocracy); and "enabler" regimes, such as the ones in Egypt and Saudi Arabia, which export their own problems with radical Islamism to other parts of the Islamic world and beyond. In this context, the task of reversing Islamist radicalism and of reforming and strengthening the state across the entire Muslim world—the Middle East and Africa, as well as South, Southeast, and Central Asia—is the greatest strategic challenge of the twenty-first century. The essential starting point is detailed knowledge of our enemy.

Thus, the working group will draw on the intellectual resources of Hoover and Stanford and on an array of scholars and practitioners from elsewhere in the United States from the Middle East and the broader world of Islam. The scholarship on contemporary Islam can now be read with discernment. A good deal of it, produced in the immediate aftermath of September 11, was not particularly deep and did not stand the test of time and events. We, however, are in the favorable position of a "second generation" assessment of that Islamic material. Our scholars and experts can report, in a detailed, authoritative way, on Islam within the Arabian Peninsula, on trends within Egyptian Islam, on the struggle between the Kemalist secular tradition in Turkey and the new Islamists, particularly the fight for the loyalty of European Islam between those who accept the canon, and the discipline, of modernism and those who do not.

Arabs and Muslims need not be believers in American exceptionalism, but our hope is to engage them in this contest of ideas. We will not necessarily aim at producing primary scholarship, but such scholarship may materialize in that our participants are researchers who know their subjects intimately. We see our critical output as essays accessible to a broader audience, primers about matters that require explication, op-eds, writings that will become part of the public debate, and short, engaging books that can illuminate the choices and the struggles in modern Islam.

We see this endeavor as a faithful reflection of the values that animate a decent, moderate society. We know the travails of modern Islam, and this working group will be unsparing in depicting them. But we also know that the battle for modern Islam is not yet lost, that there are brave men and women fighting to retrieve their faith from the extremists. Some of our participants will themselves be intellectuals and public figures who have stood up to the pressure. The working group will be unapologetic about America's role in the Muslim world. A power that laid to waste religious tyranny in Afghanistan and despotism in Iraq, that came to the rescue of the Muslims in the Balkans when they appeared all but doomed, has given much to those burdened populations. We haven't always understood Islam and Muslims—hence this inquiry. But it is a given of the working group that the pursuit of modernity and human welfare, and of the rule of law and reason, in Islamic lands is the common ground between America and contemporary Islam.

Arnold Toynbee, the once-acclaimed author of the twelve-volume *A Study of History*, wrote that the world had two geo-strategic pivots, places where an endless array of ideas and movements met, clashed, were swirled around, and then spun off to influence international affairs in all directions. One was the Oxus-Jaxartes Basin (the Pentagon today calls it Af-Pak). The other, even more extraordinary site is Syria, where civilizations and religions have jostled one another for millennia, making "a deep mark on mankind's subsequent history."

Who but Fouad Ajami could capture this Syrian uniqueness across ages and layers of political-cultural complexity? By now we can see that his oeuvre has taken shape, and works profoundly by interpreting the Arab-Islamic predicament in our time. *The*

Syrian Rebellion traces the interwoven strands of religion, politics, personalities, peace, war, revenge, and the heart-stirring aspirations of an immiserated yet valiant people—all conveyed in glimmering prose.

The Modern Age has been endowed, and tormented, by the heretofore-unknown capability of seeing all human history at a glance. We live in a "museum without walls," enabling us to recognize the signs of a world-historical moment, which is what we sense in Syria today. Ever since the march of imperial Islamic caliphates collapsed in 1924 with the end of the Ottoman Empire, the peoples of the Middle East have searched without stability or success for a Muslim identity only to be misruled by colonels, con men, retrogressive preachers, and royalist autocrats. Reform was a pipe dream; propaganda in word and intimidation in deed became the currency of life. And across these decades those outside the region could scarcely recall a time when the Middle East was neither a problem nor a threat to the rest of humankind. Thus, as the twenty-first century opened, on September 11, 2001, came the shock of recognition that only "the transformation of the greater Middle East" could keep the region from falling out of the international system, lift it from its morass, and offer it a productive role in world order and progress. The Arab Spring is an awakening to that reality by a new, youthful population self-portrayed as none of the above oppressive regimes or movements.

Syria is the cockpit or, in Toynbee's description, the "roundabout" in which all the forces face one another and spin off consequences—for good or ill—around the compass. The Syrian rebellion will be crushed, or it will gain a foothold; the latter cannot happen without outside support. The wider world must recognize that it confronts a momentous choice. If the rebels can survive without succumbing to one or another of the entrenched enemies of freedom, the transformation of the greater Middle East indeed will be under way.

Once again, Fouad Ajami does us all a signal service. Here are all the crosscurrents, all the crimes and conspiracies, all the fatuities and stratagems—and all the awakened valor of the Syrian people. They, and we, are fortunate to be guided by the author of this stunningly timely and consequential book.

CHARLES HILL

Distinguished Fellow of the Brady-Johnson
Program in Grand Strategy at Yale University;
Senior Fellow, Hoover Institution—
Co-chairman, Herbert and Jane Dwight Working Group
on Islamism and the International Order
March 2012

I HAD NOT THOUGHT that I would be writing this book. But a year into Syria's torments, the book had emerged. For nearly four decades I had had no direct access to Syria. I had older memories of it. I had grown up next door in Lebanon. My mother, in her fashion, was a believer, and the Shia shrine of Sitt Zaynab, on the outskirts of Damascus, was a place of solace for her. She thought of Zaynab—Imam Hussein's sister, who had witnessed and survived the battle of Karbala in 680—as a fellow sufferer. The shrine was a permanent place of pilgrimage for my mother, and an older sister of hers had long settled in Damascus, in a pretty house with a courtyard and a fountain. We were in and out of Damascus throughout my boyhood, in the late 1950s. I was entranced by the gardens and orchards that ringed Damascus then. And Hama, for a boy of Beirut, seemed quaint and charming, on the banks of the Orontes, with its daredevils jumping into the river from its famed waterwheels.

The legendary Egyptian Gamal Abdel Nasser had come to Damascus during that doomed union between Egypt and Syria (1958–1961). Braving my elders' wishes, I had made my own (secular) pilgrimage to see the great man, standing on a distant balcony, taking in the adoration of a Syrian crowd that was bewitched by him. Yet even then, through the haze of boyhood, there were things about Syria that could not be missed. There was a notorious prison, the Mezze, and it stood there as a forbidding reminder that this was a place that differed from our anarchic

Lebanese homeland. It took no political literacy to know that this was a country prone to intermittent seizures of power. Beirut looked to the Mediterranean; Damascus was enclosed and looked to the desert. We had Syrians in our midst, former officials, a political exile or two, married into our extended family. They had crossed the border to Lebanon, but brought with them tales of persecution and political caprice. There was Abu Abdu—an old, retired soldier. I never knew his full name. He was married to a relative of my mother. He made the best tea in our neighborhood. He had an old Syrian army coat, which gave him both warmth and something of a personal flair. Syria didn't give me much, Abu Abdu would say, only this coat. In Beirut, he never looked back on Syria. He said what he thought of it in his refusal to let his sons make the journey to his native Homs.

This book is the closing of a circle. It is an attempt to retrieve that country, so close yet so far, from books of travel and memoirs, from the daily dispatches of a people who conquered fear to challenge a despotism of unspeakable cruelty. When I stepped into the material, I found a rich literature, and I have drawn on it in this telling. My source notes will retrace my inquiry. I was lucky for the work of Patrick Seale, Albert Hourani, Hanna Batatu, Itamar Rabinovich, Philip Khoury, Marius Deeb, Martin Kramer, Daniel Pipes, Thomas Pierret, Fabrice Balanche, and Eyal Zisser. Itamar Rabinovich, a good friend of so many years, is unrivaled among the students of Syrian political history. I am truly grateful for his generosity and wisdom on the matters explored in this book. Like anyone working on Syria today, I was reliant on the rich documentation of the blog and electronic journal *Syria Comment*, a labor of love by the University of Oklahoma scholar Joshua Landis. I was lucky for the support and friendship of Professor Henry Bienen, Dr. Mark Fung, and Leon Wieseltier.

THIS IS A HOOVER BOOK, and I owe so much to many colleagues at the Hoover Institution. Hoover director John Raisian is a perfect boss, unrivaled in all my years in the academy. It was John Raisian who persuaded me to bring a teaching career to an end and join him at Hoover, to read and write. It is my hope that this work rewards his faith in me. The Shia have a unique institution, that of *marja al-taqlid* (the source of imitation). The believers defer to and imitate a learned jurist, an ayatollah they revere and to whose judgments they go for binding rulings. I have a source of imitation of my own, my Hoover colleague and legendary Yale teacher, Charles Hill. My debt to Charlie is boundless. I take great pride in the association at Hoover with former Secretary of State George P. Shultz. All of us at Hoover are in the orbit of this statesman and master of diplomacy. Secretary Shultz, in a rich and incomparable career, dealt with Syria and Lebanon. It's my hope that these pages will ring true to him.

I am indebted to my colleagues at Hoover Press—Marshall Blanchard, Jennifer Presley, Jennifer Navarrette, and their colleagues—for their dedication to producing the best of books. Their patience, their skills, and their innate understanding of how to bring a manuscript to fruition make one glad as an author to have come knocking at their door. Denise Elson has been from the beginning our cheerleader. Her great spirit, wise words, and encouragement have followed every step of this book, as they did a dozen earlier Hoover books and working papers with which I have been associated. Jeff Jones has been with us from the launch of our working group, and we value his dedication and commitment to our project. I could not have hoped for a more attentive and subtle a copy editor as Ms. Oie Lian Yeh. This book is better for her collaboration.

This book follows a dozen Hoover books and long papers done under the auspices of the Herbert and Jane Dwight Working Group on Islamism and the International Order, and behind these two names are the best of patrons and allies who believed in the need to understand the Greater Middle East and its contemporary ordeal.

I HAVE LEFT TO THE END my trusted colleague, Megan Ring. Megan is an original. There is no source she can't track down, no demand she can't fulfill. We have worked together on previous books and scores of essays. She now coordinates the Herbert and Jane Dwight Working Group on Islamism and the International Order. At first glance, the word "coordinate" doesn't fit this woman of free spirit. But all those who have worked with her know better. She is a consummate performer of tasks.

The dedication is for Leila Deluca Ajami, my beloved granddaughter. Watching the pain of Syria, I saw children her age, boys and girls of five or six, holding placards and waving Syrian flags, carried atop the shoulders of their parents. I knew Leila was safe in Brooklyn with her parents. They weren't in Homs and Deraa. But for the children there, I thought I owed them a humble chronicle of their grief—and hopes.

FOUAD AJAMI
March 2012

THE SYRIAN
REBELLION

Oh people,
I have become sultan over you
Smash your idols after a long darkness
Worship me.
Every time I thought of abdicating power
my conscience devoured me.
Who, after me, will rule the good people?
Who, after me, will cure the lame,
the cripple, the leper, the blind?
And who will summon the dead back to life?
Who will bring the people the rain?
Who will administer to them ninety lashes
who will crucify them on the trees
who will force them to live like cattle?
And die like cattle?
Every time I thought of leaving them
my tears overflowed
I trusted my fate to God
and I decided to ride this people
from now until Judgment Day.

—Syrian poet Nizar Qabbani, "The Autobiography of an Arab Man of the Sword"

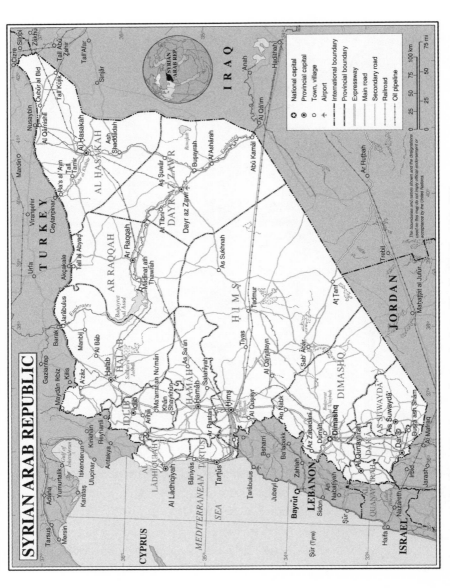

Source: United Nations, Dept. of Field Support, Cartographic Section: Map No. 4204 Rev. 2, May 2008.

CHAPTER ONE

Prologue:
The Inheritor

This is as follows: The builder of the family's glory knows what it cost him to do the work, and he keeps the qualities that created his glory and made it last. The son who comes after him had personal contact with his father and thus learned those things from him. However, he is inferior to him in this respect, inasmuch as a person who learns things through study is inferior to a person who knows them from practical application.

THE GREAT NORTH AFRICAN HISTORIAN, Ibn Khaldun (1332–1406), wrote the above of dynasties in his *Muqaddimah: An Introduction to History*. Ibn Khaldun had written that prestige in one lineage lasts four generations before it dissipates. It is doubtful whether the Assad lineage is slated for four generations. What mattered as a rebellion broke out in Syria in 2011 was the insight to the relation— the similarities, the difference in skills—between Hafez al-Assad and his son Bashar. The father had rigged the succession; fear had done the trick. The lieutenants in the wings, old subordinates and colleagues who had known the father and who had ideas of their own that his death would give them a shot at succession, were bullied and sidelined. There was Vice President Abdul Halim Khaddam, a lawyer from Baniyas and a Sunni who was

two years younger than Hafez al-Assad, an ally from the very
beginning of the Assad reign. There was Minister of Defense
Mustafa Tlas, also a Sunni, from Rastan, near Homs. He had
served in that position since 1972 and hailed from the officer
class, unfailingly loyal to his leader. These and others had been
pushed aside in favor of a newly minted "General" Bashar al-
Assad, thirty-four-years old when he inherited the realm. This
was not the script that the ruler had had in mind. He had
groomed his oldest son, Basel. But that son had died in a traffic
accident in 1994. The old guard had to submit to and accept this
dynastic succession. Khaddam didn't and ended up making his
way to exile and opposition from Paris. Hafez al-Assad didn't
have much time to tutor Bashar, and as Ibn Khaldun and countless others had told us, such skills are not easy to transmit.

"*Yalla Erhal Ya Bashar*" ("Come on Bashar, Leave"), the
crowds had taken to chanting. More poignantly, in Hama, the
young people carried placards that read, "Like Father, Like Son."
Back when he had come into power, Bashar had made a good
first impression, if only because he was different from his intim-
idating, stern father. His father had been a peasant boy, born in
the Alawi mountains and married into his own community; he
had come into the coastal city of Latakia, and he had plotted
his way to the summit of political power. So many of Hafez
al-Assad's peers and rivals had fallen to assassins' bullets or perished in Syria's cruel prisons, dispatched there by Assad himself.
In contrast, Bashar had been the entitled prince, schooled in the
best academies in Damascus and with a stint of time in London
behind him. He had known no hardship. In the manner of a
society eager for deliverance, it was hoped that he would open up
the big prison that Syria had become under his father.

Outsiders prophesied good tidings for Bashar. U.S. Secretary
of State Madeleine Albright, who had gone to the Old Man's

funeral in 2000 and met the son, came back with a favorable report: he was a "reformer," she said, bent on modernizing his country. French President Jacques Chirac took it upon himself to induct the young ruler into the respectable order of nations. Bashar married well, which was his first olive branch to his country. His wife was a Sunni, the London-born daughter of a cardiologist, Fawwaz al-Akhras, who lived in self-imposed exile in London and spoke discreetly of the sins of the old regime. The bride had worked for J. P. Morgan in London and was on her way to pursue a Harvard MBA when she met and then married Bashar. There was talk of a "Damascus Spring" at the beginning of his reign.

Small gestures mattered. Bashar made his way to restaurants now and then without heavy security. He was head of the Syria Computer Society and promised openness in a country where the ownership of fax machines was restricted. Western cigarettes, banned by his father, were now available. There was a boom in tourism and a respectable flow of investments from the Gulf states. Art galleries and five-star hotels changed the drab atmosphere. He released from captivity several hundred political prisoners, and his people could be forgiven the classic hope that if only the "good tsar" knew, if only his palace guard would let him rule according to his wishes, the realm would be repaired and the oppression lifted. But the realm was what it was, the political universe had been closed up. Power had made a seamless transition—from the Baath Party to the Alawis, and then to the House of Assad—from the sect to the family. The young man who was said to thrill to the music of Phil Collins was cut of the old cloth. He, too, like his father, could brook no dissent.

Syrians had puzzled over their ruler's place in the constellation of power: was he, like his father before him, master of the realm, or a puppet, his strings pulled by mightier powers? To rule Syria

effectively, the man at the helm had to have mastery over the four
pillars of political power—the Alawite community, the army, the
security services, the Baath Party. A renowned journalist and
activist, Michel Kilo would maintain as late as 2009 that Bashar
dominated foreign policy while the security services reigned over
domestic affairs. The answer as to the proclivities of the young
ruler was not long in coming. The regime quickly snuffed out
the Damascus Spring. There was a thirst for liberty. Syrians long
silenced yearned for political argument and debate, it had been so
prominent a feature of their political life before the Assad years.
A noted intellectual and academic living and teaching in Paris,
Burhan Ghalioun recalls the enthusiasm of that moment: civic
forums sprouted everywhere, there were fifty new "salons" in the
space of a few months, and even villages wanted forums of their
own and were willing to run afoul of the security forces. Ghalioun
attributes this enthusiasm to the "exceptional thirst of the Syrian
middle class for freedom." One such civic group, the Forum for
National Dialogue, headed by Riad Seif, a dissident of high
standing and genuine courage, invited Ghalioun to give a public
lecture. Seven hundred people showed up, and Baath Party functionaries grew alarmed at the public ferment. People had taken
the young president's claims to openness at face value and had
begun to test them. It did not really matter whether the ruler
himself had recognized the threats to the autocracy, or whether
that perennial "old guard" had drawn a line against these new
temptations. The forums were shut down, and dissidents hauled
off to prison were given sentences between two and ten years. "I
called it a warm day in winter," a renowned civil libertarian and
lawyer, Haitham al-Maleh, said of this false spring. "I was not
surprised. Bashar is the son of his father." The hopes invested in
the young ruler were in vain. If anything, Bashar's rearing had

formed an uncompromising autocrat, one perhaps more unyielding than his father. Ghalioun put it well: "When Assad the elder died, I knew his son was going to be more dangerous than his father. His father was a political figure with political connections. He had struggled to reach his position, irrespective of his methods. But Bashar was born into a *qawqaa* (a shell), with no political experience. I knew he would not be able to respond to a complex society and that he would use violence more than his father. People would say he is more open, European-educated. But I viewed him as a young, inexperienced, out-of-touch crown prince, surrounded by bodyguards and an entourage."

There came a time when the guesswork about the ruler subsided. This "crown prince" had been bequeathed his kingdom by autocracy—his father's will, the accidental death of his older brother, Basel, who had been groomed to rule—and it stood to reason that he would defend what he had been given.

An irresistible force has clashed with an immovable object. The regime could not frighten the population, and the people could not dispatch the highly entrenched regime that Assad Senior had built, the most fearsome national security state in the Arab East. In other words, a country confronting the classic ingredients of a civil war, and a sectarian war within. The Syrians who braved it all did not want to be ruled by Bashar's children in the way they had been ruled by Bashar and their parents by Bashar's father. As though to foreclose the political universe, Bashar had a son and named him Hafez. The age-old bargain in Arab lands, bread for freedom, had come apart in Syria, more than 30 percent of its people were living below the poverty line, and key sectors of the economy were in the hands of the House of Assad and their in-laws. A proud people wanted something more than this drab regime of dictatorship and plunder.

Hitherto quiescent people were done with the Assad tyranny, and they were ready to pay the ultimate price. The dictatorship alternated savage violence with promises of reform. The protests had begun in mid-March, and the regime was to make what it saw as its big concession—the lifting of the emergency law that had governed the country since 1963. But the tanks and the helicopter gunships were now loose on the population. Syrians were fleeing across the borders to Turkey and Jordan and Lebanon. Amid this violence, the ruler appeared dazed and uncertain. He could not recognize the rebellious people demanding an end to his tyranny. For four long decades, the Assad dynasty, the intelligence barons, and the brigade commanders had grown accustomed to a culture of quiescence and silence. Ruler and ruled were now in uncharted territory. A boy of thirteen from the southern town of Deraa, by the Jordanian border, Hamza al-Khatib would emerge as the emblematic figure of this war between the regime and its people. The boy had been picked up along with a number of his peers. They had committed the unpardonable sin of scribbling anti-regime graffiti on their town walls. His body was returned to his family a month later. He had been subjected to horrific torture, his knees and neck broken, even his genitals severed. In the mind of the dictatorship and its enforcers, this was meant to do the trick and scare people into their private homes. It had worked that way before, but the barrier of fear was broken. That grim deed had strengthened the resolve of those who wanted to be done with the cruel regime. Another notable crime took place in Hama and it was to echo through the country: the body of a young cement layer named Ibrahim Qashoush was dragged from the Orontes River in July. The man's throat had been cut and his vocal cords ripped out. Torturers and regime enforcers are never subtle. The man had sinned against the order of things by singing a popular protest lyric, *"Yalla Erhal Ya Bashar"* ("Come on Bashar, Leave"). The silence had been breached, and a lyric would cost a man his life. Clarity came with the repression. The protesters were now saying that they hated the regime and its functionaries more than they did the Israelis they had long hated and maligned. Those with a memory of their country under French rule—and young protesters who were told of this history—now spoke of the respect shown by French forces for the sanctity of mosques. Mosques were then off-limits, a sanctuary for protesters on the run. Now mosques, and even their prayer leaders, were fair targets for the forces of the regime.

It's no surprise the eruption came in Syria, chronologically, after the upheavals of Tunisia, Egypt, Yemen, Libya, and Bahrain. The Syrians had taken their time. It was as though a people knew that they were in for a particularly grim and bloody struggle. Tunisia had led the caravan and then stepped out of the way, its upheaval overwhelmed by the protests in Cairo. The Tunisian strongman had made a run for it first, on January 14, 2011. The Egyptian ruler had followed, his reign of three decades coming to an end on February 11. Libya, flanked to the west by Tunisia and in the shadow of Egypt to the east, rose in rebellion on February 17. The date would become, on the calendar of the Libyan rebels, the birth of their new order.

Fittingly, Friday would become the big day of protest. The protesters would give each Friday a name and a theme—Your Silence Is Killing Us, the Friday for International Protection, the Friday of the Free Syrian Army, With Us Is God, and so forth. Forty-two Fridays were to come and go in 2011, and both the regime and the opposition were standing their ground. Bashar, the accidental inheritor of a political realm, now had his own war. He had stepped out of his father's shadow only to merge with it.

If the protesters were discouraged, they didn't show it. They vowed that 2012 would see the end of this dictatorship.

From Ibn Khaldun:

> *As one can see, we have these three generations. In the course of these three generations, the dynasty grows servile and is worn out. Therefore, it is in the fourth generation that ancestral prestige is destroyed.*

Bashar al-Assad did not have to worry about the two generations to come after him squandering ancestral prestige. Ibn Khaldun was a genius, but history moved with velocity nowadays. This dynastic inheritance in Syria was not destined to survive the second generation.

Ibn Khaldun may have been excessively generous with the life span he gave dynasties—from their rise from "savage," austere beginnings to their descent into ease, luxury, and dissolution. But the great gift of his analysis, and one that unlocks the Syrian present—and so much of political life in the Arab-Islamic domains—was the central notion of *asabiyah* (solidarity, group feeling, group consciousness). The great North African observer of history saw asabiyah as central to the rise of dynasties and to the building of a *dawla* (state). "Royal authority and large-scale dynastic power are attained only through a group and group feeling. This is because aggressive and defensive strength is obtained only through group feeling, which means affection and willingness to fight and die for each other." It was possible, he wrote, to establish royal domination without "religious coloring," but only barely so. The norm was group feeling buttressed by one of religious propaganda. Here is his central proposition: "Religious propaganda gives a dynasty at its beginning another power in addition to that of the group feeling it possessed as a result of the number of its supporters." Alawi asabiyah made this Assad regime—the group feeling of a mountain people who had a jumbled mix of persecution and superiority hammered into them by history. It is perfectly consistent and rational for a people to suffer material destitution while still entertaining notions of their superiority to people of means and leisure, and this was at the heart of the antagonism between the Alawi mountain and the Sunni cities. But there was another maxim favored and frequently used by Ibn Khaldun—the common people always follow the religion of their rulers. "The vanquished always want to imitate the victor in his distinctive characteristics, his dress, his occupation, and all his other conditions and customs."

This was where the Syrian edifice would crack. There was no possibility that the Syrian populace—Islamically devout and in the midst of an Arab-Islamic world awakening to the power of Islam—would follow a community of schismatics. There were cases of young Sunni students in universities, observers tell us, imitating the distinctive speech of the Alawi mountain and coastland. But they were the exceptions. The Alawi dominion was not destined to last. Bashar surely lacked the cunning of his father, but the Alawi odyssey carried within it the seeds of its own destruction.

Next door in Lebanon, the Maronites, another mountain people with an asabiyah of their own, had enjoyed primacy. But their condition and their relation to the communities with which they shared the small country couldn't have been more different. The Maronite mountain was never an isolated world. The Mediterranean and their national church gave the Maronites wide cultural and political horizons. The Maronite patriarchs recognized the supremacy of Rome in the late years of the twelfth century. Though the Holy See had not always been attentive to this remote people, the religious traffic had enriched the life of the Maronites. A Maronite college in Rome, established in the sixteenth century, trained young clerics in the Roman ecclesiastical doctrine. The Maronites were to prove a gifted people. The literary renaissance in Arabic letters, the so-called age of enlightenment, *asr al-nahda*, in the late 1800s rested in large measure on the superb abilities of the Maronite writers. It's true that France had given Maronites favored treatment during the Mandate years. But the Maronites made their own luck when the French quit Lebanon.

The first Lebanese republic (1943–1975) was anchored in a Maronite-Sunni entente. The Maronites did not govern alone, and they didn't rule by force of arms. Their primacy, if they had it, issued out of their superior educational achievements; their schools were the pride of the country, the destination of choice for the gifted and ambitious young Muslims. There were the lands of *al-mahjar* (the diaspora communities) in North and South America, and the Maronites were dominant there. From al-mahjar came ideas, social capital, and repatriated wealth. In the Lebanon of the 1950s and 1960s (if I may be permitted a side note of autobiography from my boyhood), the Maronites were envied and admired, and covertly imitated by the other communities. Their schools and monasteries were the institutions of a people proud of their accomplishments. None of this holds true for the Alawis. There was no diaspora that knit them into a bigger world. There was the military and, in time, the Baath Party that brought them out of their solitude.

CHAPTER TWO

Come the Mountain People

H ISTORY HAD BEEN UNKIND to the Alawis—their theology perhaps mattered less than their sociology. They
were an insular mountain community, impoverished
and disdained by the peoples of the cities and plains. They had
emerged as a schism within Shiism more than a millennium ago.
It was in a tumultuous century—the closing years of the ninth
century to the middle of the tenth—that the sect appeared. Mainstream (Twelver) Shiism was in crisis: the eleventh imam had died
and his infant son, designated as the *mahdi* (the redeemer), had
vanished before the eyes of ordinary men to return at the "end of
time" and fill the earth with justice. Pretenders rose amid this
uncertainty, and charismatic preachers filled the void, working
their will and conceptions on religious dogma. The adherents of
this sect moved between Iraq and Syria, and then made their
home in the massive mountain range in northern Syria. For several centuries they went by the name of Nusayris and gave their
name to the mountain range they inhabited. Their principal theo-
logian, a preacher by the name of Abdullah al-Khasibi, proclaimed the divinity of Imam Ali, the Prophet's cousin and
son-in-law. Theirs was a syncretistic theology that included Neo-
platonic, Gnostic, Christian, Muslim, and Zoroastrian elements.
For both Sunni and Shia Muslims alike, the Nusayris were *ghulat*
(extremist) exaggerators who carried the veneration of Ali beyond
the bounds of Islam.

A thorough study of the heterodox Shia cults, Matti Moosa's *Extreme Shiites: The Ghulat Sects* sets the place of Imam Ali in the cosmology of the Nusayris: "To the Nusayris, Ali Ibn Abi Talib, blood cousin and son-in-law of the Prophet Muhammad, is the last and only perfect one of the seven manifestations of God, in which the Islamic religion and its Sharia law have been revealed. He is the one who created Muhammad and taught him the Quran. He is the fountainhead of Islam. He is God, the very God of the Quran." The break with Islam is total. To the Sunnis, Ali was one of the four Guided Caliphs (successors to the Prophet), husband of Muhammad's daughter Fatima, father of the Prophet's grandchildren. His place in the order and the history of Islam is secure and beyond reproach. To the Shia, Imam Ali is the beloved man around whom Shiism had crystallized. He had been robbed of his right to inherit the Prophet's mantle, he had been made to wait for his turn at leadership, and three caliphs had gone before him. He had come to his caliphate during a great schism, a civil war within the new community of Islam, and an assassin had taken his life in 661, a mere five years into his reign. Then there was the cruel fate and disinheritance of his progeny— the canonical martyrdom of his son, Hussein, at Karbala in southern Iraq two decades later. Ali is beloved to the Shia, but he takes his place next to the Prophet, by his side, always subordinate, and never deified. The Nusayris were a religion apart.

One of the most influential jurists in orthodox Islamic history, Ibn Taymiyyah (1263–1328) branded the Nusayris as sectarians outside the faith. Ibn Taymiyyah had come into his own in the aftermath of the Mongol destruction of Baghdad in 1258. The Sunni international order was in disrepair, and for Ibn Taymiyyah the faith was imperiled. He grew up in Damascus and emerged as the uncompromising defender of Sunni orthodoxy. As the political journalist Nibras Kazimi put it in his study of 2010, *Syria through Jihadist Eyes: A Perfect Enemy*, jihadists in our time have turned to Ibn Taymiyyah for "succor and guidance" for they see this moment of Islam's ordeal as a repetition of that time of trouble. No comfort to the Alawis then and now, Ibn Taymiyyah saw these sectarians as enemies of Islam. "Their religion externally is Shiism but internally it is pure unbelief," the jurist wrote. A scold and a zealot, Ibn Taymiyyah issued severe fatwas against the Nusayris that left no room for compromise. Their blood and wealth were permissible for the taking: they were apostates who had to be punished, even exterminated, wherever they were found.

Taqiyya (dissimulation and concealment) was essential to a faith at odds with Islamic orthodoxy. And a mountain abode was the safe and rightful place to live and practice the faith. The Nusayris had footholds in Baghdad and Aleppo, but those were quickly lost. The Ottomans, who found Nusayris in their isolation when they conquered Syria in the sixteenth century, dubbed them *al-milla al-dhalla* (the lost nation). It had been idle to try to bring them into the fold, and the Ottomans, an expedition or two aside, left them unmolested. The chroniclers who knew the Nusayris tell of a people riven by conflicts and their veritable wasteland of a country.

There is an indelible portrait of this community at mid-nineteenth century in one of the remarkable books of travel and Western missionary writings, *The Land and the Book*, by W. M. Thomson. Thomson was, in his own words, "thirty years missionary in Syria and Palestine." He was an American and penned this book in 1857. He was an impatient man. He loved the land of Syria and Palestine, treasured its flora and fauna, and rendered it with exacting detail, but he had no patience for the

people. They were an unbearable lot, and they were living heed-
less in the land of the revelation. In one of his journeys through
the land, he comes to the country of the Nusayris. They are a
puzzle to him, so "peculiar in physiognomy," so "unlike the Arabs
as to indicate a different origin." It was impossible to ascertain
their number, but they had "more than a thousand villages and
hamlets, and have been estimated as high as two hundred thousand." He had no fondness for them as he knew them from prior
travels among them. "Their religion is a profound secret, but is
believed to be more famous than their external morals. The skill
with which they evade any approximation toward their religious
mysteries always excited my astonishment." What sort of people
inhabited these mountains, Thomson inquired of an elderly man
of this community. "Oh, they are *fellaheen*." Thomson already
knew they were peasants, he was inquiring about their faith.
"Religion! said he; What need have fellaheen of religion?"
Thomson was nothing if not persistent. What prophet do you
follow, he asked his informant. "We rather love Ali. . . . We also
love Jesus Christ and curse Mohammed. You and we are one."
This remark about Muhammad and Jesus Christ was offered after
Thomson himself had said that he was Christian, he loved Jesus
Christ, and "our religion is contained in the New Testament."
"But enough of the Nusayris for the present," Thomson wrote.
No secrets had been divulged to him, and the people of this
mountain had kept him at bay.

The cruelty of their history and the harsh poverty had forced
many of the Nusayris in the course of the nineteenth century to
move down to the plains, to till the land for absentee landlords in
Latakia and the province of Hama. Always go down, never go up,
went an expression of mountain life, and the Nusayris did just
that. The Nusayris had always bristled under the name given

them by outsiders. It was in the opening years of the twentieth century that they were to be known by their preferred name, the Alawis.

More than a favorable change of names came the way of the Alawis with the destruction of the Ottoman Empire. The French Mandate that took in Syria and Lebanon arrived with an explicit minorities policy. The Sunni Muslims had lost a world, the Ottoman Empire had been a dominion of orthodox Islam, and the most humble of townsmen in Hama or Aleppo could see his faith in the practice and creed of the state. The majority of the Sunnis wanted nothing to do with the new French masters. France had blown in and out of their world as a protector of the Catholics of the Ottoman Empire. Its missions and philanthropies, its consular protection, had been gifts to its Catholic wards. In truth, the French had been allies of the Ottoman sultanate, but that was now forgotten. At any rate, that intimacy with the Ottoman rulers had stirred the jealousies of the Muslim notables and traders. France was not at the zenith of its power, and the minorities policy it utilized was recognition of that weakness. It was a policy of divide and rule. Greater Syria was divided into four political units: the Lebanese republic, the republic of Syria, the state of the Alawis (later renamed the government of Latakia), and the government of Jebel Druze. The state of the Alawis was a natural unit, Jebel Ansariyah, the mountain range and home of the Alawis and the coastal plain at its foot—with the town of Latakia its principal urban center. In *Syria and Lebanon: A Political Essay*, the historian Albert Hourani writes that this state had a population of approximately 370,000. Of this number, 60 percent were Alawis, 20 percent Sunnis, and the rest divided among Ismailis and various Christian denominations. Alawi sentiment savored this autonomy and wanted to keep the

Syrian nationalists in Damascus at bay. Hourani put it well: France had "made articulate the corporate consciousness" of the minorities. She had not created it; she had simply given expression to it in her administrative organization.

The gift of autonomy that France extended the Alawis—and the Druze—could not last. In 1936, a Franco-Syrian treaty brought the autonomy of these two communities to an end. The urban elites in Damascus had their way, and the French could not keep the promise they had made to the minorities. This history would remain the stuff of controversy. The nationalist elites in Damascus would write it the standard, expected way: the national will had prevailed, the scheme of an outside power foiled. But it was a messier history: there was no uniform opinion in the Alawi mountain or the Jebel Druze—or among the Kurds in the Jazirah, Syria's eastern hinterland. There were unionists who welcomed the new order. They were drawn by the pull of Syrian nationalism, and no doubt they came to that sentiment out of a realistic reading of France's own ambivalence and hesitations. But the weight of preference, it is fair to say, was in favor of autonomy under French protection. The intermittent disturbances among the Alawis, the Druze, and the Kurds highlighted the tension among these communities and the nationalism of the towns. The minorities looked at this new doctrine with a jaundiced eye. They had no faith that the urban elites would grant them justice and regard. For substantial majorities in the compact communities, this nationalism was a cover for Sunni domination.

The meticulous work of historian Itamar Rabinovich cuts through this tangled history with detailed evidence and precision. Direct French rule in the Alawi areas, established in 1921, had been "orderly and efficient, enjoyed local cooperation, and the reforms it introduced resulted in a noticeable improvement of the standard of living." The dominant sentiment among the Alawis was separatism. The Alawis savored their "isolation from Damascus and Hama and their share of government positions in their own territory." The Druze mountain was almost exclusively Druze in its demographic composition, and the Alawi territory had a substantial Sunni presence to contend with. The town of Latakia was the political capital of the Alawis; but it had been, as Rabinovich reminds us, the seat of the local Ottoman governor, and many Alawis there served as sharecroppers to Sunni land-lords. The Alawi subordination was more extreme in Hama and its rural hinterland: "Anti-Sunni sentiment among the Alawis was therefore not an abstract resentment of a remote political center but a very concrete grudge." The isolation and poverty engendered among the Alawis a "strong feeling of solidarity with an attachment to the community and a sense of exclusiveness and mission."

A petition sent to Leon Blum, the head of the Popular Front government, and signed by six Alawi notables laid out the case for Alawi independence under French tutelage. The Alawis were an independent people. They had never been "subject to the authority of the cities of the interior," the petitioners wrote. The parliamentary rule promised by the nationalists was nothing more than "false appearances without any value." A "spirit of hatred and fanaticism imbedded in the hearts of the Arab Muslims against everything that is non-Muslim" held out for the Alawis nothing but the threat of dominion and "annihilation."

Remarkably enough in light of what the future would bring in the fight for Palestine, the petitioners pointed to that struggle as evidence of the militancy of Islam against those who don't belong to it. Those "good Jews" in Palestine had "contributed to the Arabs with civilization and peace, scattered gold, and established

prosperity in Palestine without harming anyone or taking anything by force, yet the Muslims declared holy war against them
and never hesitated in killing their women and children, despite
the presence of England in Palestine and France in Syria. Therefore, a dark fate awaits the Jews and other minorities in case the
Mandate is abolished, and Muslim Syria is united with Muslim
Palestine. The union of the two countries is the ultimate goal of
the Muslim Arabs." Treaties would not protect the minorities,
the petitioners warned. "We assure you that treaties have no value
in relation to the Islamic mentality in Syria. We have previously
seen this situation in the Anglo-Iraqi treaty, which did not pre-
vent the Iraqis from slaughtering the Assyrians and the Yezidis."

Two of the signatories are of particular interest. The first was
Sulayman al-Murshid, a sheepherder and an epileptic, who
emerged in a remote mountain village preaching the "end of the
world" and claiming that he had received heavenly messages. In
no time he claimed divinity for himself, a self-styled god holding
out redemption for the needy and the afflicted. He acquired a
huge following among his Alawi kinsmen and, in the process,
unsettled the religious class. A voracious bandit, he came into
possession of vast tracts of land and countless concubines. He
alternately befriended the French and fought against them. In
urban Syria, he was loathed as a pretender and a traitor. He got
himself elected to the parliament. Ten years after this petition,
the powers in Damascus sent him to the gallows.

The second signatory, by contrast, was a silent figure, a peasant
by the name of Sulayman al-Assad. He had some standing in his
village of Qardaha and was a strict disciplinarian with his children. A son of his, Hafez, would make his way to the coastal city
of Latakia, student activism, the military academy, and the apex
of political power. Sulayman al-Assad, petitioning the mandatory

power against a united Syria, couldn't have imagined what triumph awaited his kin.

This petition and other Alawi entreaties to the French were in vain. The Syrian polity that would emerge out of French rule would include the territory of the Alawis, the Druze, and the Kurds. In retrospect, the Syrian nationalists in the principal cities were given more than they could keep. In their historiography, there was grief at what had been lost in the making of Greater Lebanon. The newly created Lebanese entity was to include the Bekaa Valley, the Shia stronghold in the south, and the coastal cities of Tripoli, Beirut, and Sidon. There was also the trauma of loss with the annexation of the Alexandretta province and its port, and the city of Antioch, to Turkey in 1939. This province had a mixed population of Alawis, Christians, Armenians, and Turks. The Kemalist regime in Ankara was bent on annexing it, and France had given way.

The urban elites who dominated the politics of this emerging Syrian state were in no mood for compromise with the minorities and the hinterland. Sunni governors were sent to the Druze and Alawi areas, and a powerful myth of the "Arabism" of Syria and its population served to further marginalize the minorities. As Itamar Rabinovich put it, the "unionist" elites insisted that there was nothing particularistic or different about the Alawis—or the Druze and the Kurds for that matter. They were Syrians, like all the others, true Arabs and Muslims who simply "lagged behind." Granted time and education, they would be assimilated into the mainstream.

When the scales were tipped in favor of those among the Alawis who had accepted a place in the Syrian state, a gift came their way through the auspices of the mufti of Jerusalem, Hajj Amin al-Husseini. A political man through and through, he saw religion as a weapon and a mask. The mufti issued an edict in the summer of 1936 that the Alawis were indeed Muslims and "ought to be wholeheartedly accepted by every Muslim." The heretics were now dubbed Muslim Alawis. The mufti's horizons were always pan-Arab, and this edict couldn't have been a big concern of his. It was issued in July 1936, at a time when a ferocious rebellion engulfed the Palestinians. The Arab Rebellion would rage for three years and drown the Palestinians in blood and misery. The mufti was a protagonist in that struggle, the most extreme and violent of the contenders. He had enemies nearby to take on, and that edict on the Alawis couldn't have detained him long.

The political wind was blowing the way of the (Sunni) centralizers in the cities. French authority had lent its coattails to the minorities, but that authority was devastated by the fall of Paris to the Nazis. Britain would come to acquire greater latitude in the Levant—the Free French relied entirely on British power. British policy was uncompromising in its support for the unity of Syria and its nationalist leaders. From the vantage point of the soldiers and diplomats who ran Britain's affairs in the Levant, the Alawis were but a cat's-paw of a French design to reassert direct French authority over Syria. The urban elites had grown confident that the new polity was theirs. In Rabinovich's words, "self confidence also bred obtuseness to the anxieties of the minorities and underlay a policy which sought to integrate and fully assimilate the Druze and Alawi areas into the Syrian state."

There was one gift, though, that the French bequeathed the Alawis that would endure and dictate the course of the Syrian polity. The French had recruited heavily among the minorities for their Troupes Speciales du Levant. The Alawis had taken to this path out of poverty. Military service provided steady pay and respectability, a new life beyond the desperate mountain villages. The Sunnis disdained military service and could do without it. A mere two decades after independence, the military would overturn the rule of the Sunni notables and bureaucratic class. The political order was there for the plucking, and the new men, the desolation of the countryside perilously close to them, had nothing to lose. The order of centuries had been more feeble than the soldiers and ideologues could have imagined.

This transformation was nothing less than a violation of the order of things. In a definitive study, political historian Martin Kramer gave this radical rupture its proper reading: the Alawis, once peasants, had "beaten their ploughshares into swords, first becoming military officers, then using the instruments of war to seize the state." To the Sunnis, this was "usurpation," Kramer writes. "Syria was their patrimony," they had admitted the Alawis into the national project, and now the stepchildren had become masters of the domain. "Alawi ascendance left the Sunnis disillusioned, betrayed by the ideology of Arabism which they themselves had concocted." There was a supreme irony at work, and Kramer writes: "The Alawis, having been denied their own state by the Sunni nationalists, had taken all of Syria instead. Arabism, once a convenient device to reconcile minorities to Sunni rule, now was used to reconcile Sunnis to the rule of minorities." Pity the artisans, small traders, and religious functionaries in the warrens of Hama and Damascus: a heterodox sect of peasants had conquered their homeland. They had once defined the nation in secular terms; they would now seek to redefine it along religious lines and put the Alawis beyond the pale.

CHAPTER THREE

The Time of the Founder

P OLITICAL POWER in this new Syria issued out of the bar-
rel of a gun, of course. But ideology, above all that of the
Baath Party, played its role—it gave the new men the
language they needed to cover up personal and sectarian ambitions. Three Baathist military seizures of power altered beyond
recognition the Syrian political landscape—the first came in
1963, the second in 1966, the third in 1970. The concentration
of power grew more extreme in the course of this tumultuous
period, as did the sectarianism. The first coup d'état was a jumbled mix of ideological drive and ambition, the coming together
of Baathist officers and ideologues to upend an old order of privilege. Men of rural origins—Ismailis, Druze, Alawis, and Sunnis
from the lower rungs of that community—had pulled off that
coup. There had been a welter of ideological movements battling
for this country's direction—Nasserists, communists, believers in
greater Syrian nationalism—but the Baath had prevailed. It was
in that formative period that the emergency decrees which would
remain the law of the land for the next six decades were enunci-
ated. The "historic" founders of Baathism, Michel Aflaq and
Salah al-Din al-Bitar, who had conceived their ideology in Paris
in the interwar years, had gotten what they wanted. They had
penetrated the officer corps, they had secured the defeat of the
"feudalists" and the big families, they had shown up the Egyptian

leader Gamal Abdel Nasser, and they had pushed aside rival political parties.

The second coup, three years later, was a conspiracy within a conspiratorial party. The founders were pushed aside—the legendary Aflaq was expelled from the party he conceived. He would quit Syria for good and memorably proclaim that this Baath was not his Baath and that these soldiers were not his soldiers. A younger, more parochial breed had risen to power. Two Alawi officers, Salah Jadid and Hafez al-Assad, now dominated the military/Baathist edifice. Those two men and the officers who clustered around them had not known the culture and the ways of the Syrian cities, let alone those of Paris. Ideologically, this was a hard-line regime that was hostile to merchants and private enterprise at home, and fierce and reckless in pan-Arab and regional affairs. This was the regime that would for all intents and purposes trigger the Six-Day War of 1967. The sectarianism of the regime was now barely concealed: the Alawis cast aside the Druze and the Ismaili officers, but they left some room for those among the Sunnis willing to accept the reality of Alawi power. But this second Baathist regime was doomed from within: a struggle between Hafez al-Assad and Salah Jadid was settled in favor of the former. Jadid had taken off his uniform and based his power in the party apparatus; Assad, more shrewd, had opted to remain within the military and the officer corps. His seizure of power was put forth as a "corrective movement" against Salah Jadid and the hard-liners.

This coup d'état in 1970 put an end to the cycle of military seizures of power that had punctuated Syrian politics since the first coup in 1949. The new ruler would give his country stability, but at a terrible price. It hadn't taken long for the more discerning in this political-military class, from within the ranks of the Baath at that, to voice their sense of disappointment and betrayal. There had been the philosopher-king of the Baath, Michel Aflaq, disowning his political children. But by far the best autopsy of what had befallen this new order came from the pen of one of its most distinguished minds, Sami al-Jundi, and it came as early as 1969. His book *Al-Baath*, published in Beirut, must be reckoned as one of the classics of its genre in Arabic political memoirs. Born in 1921 in the town of Salamiyah, near Hama, Sami al-Jundi hailed from an Ismaili family of immense learning. He had held a cabinet position in the first Baath government in 1963–64. He had been sent abroad as ambassador to France a year or two later. A dentist by training, he was a lyricist of delicate touch and an unillusioned man who was above dissimulation and doublespeak. He had known both imprisonment and high office.

To the odyssey of the Baath, he had brought a lover's disillusionment. The Baath had been his world, and it had grown strange and unfamiliar to him. "Who would have thought in the year of 1940–1941 that the Baath would end with all this waste? Who among us would have predicted that the label of being called a Baathist would become an accusation that we would deny with such bitterness? No one today would believe that we once had a cause, for they insist that we are informers, writers of reports, wielders of the whip, and killers. People nowadays accuse us of treason, go so far as dismissing everything we said as hypocrisy and opportunism. At the beginning people thought we were a new phenomenon—serious, idealistic. They never believed that we were playing with fire." Power had led to ruin. "Our journey to power was quick, brief, and dangerous. Our generation never thought that we would come to rule. We found ourselves in positions of authority, with a new mentality but with old methods, lacking both experience and ideology." The young cadres of the

Baath were convinced that "the age of decline had come to an end with the demise of the old politicians and that we are the dawn of a new culture. We turned out to be but the latest version of backwardness."

Of his companions, Jundi would say that they had lived "the foolishness of the true believers." They were poor but paid no heed to that, they read widely, and they were drawn to Germanic ideas of nationalism. It had all been a swindle. The Baath had acquired all its aura and brilliance holding up the cause of Palestine, and now there it stood, after 1967, responsible for the "most humiliating and catastrophic defeat in Arab history." They were given their chance because Syrians had grown convinced that the political class that had fought for independence could not answer the yearnings of a new generation. Out of the tumult of the 1940s—the end of the French Mandate, the coming of national independence in 1946—the Baath had emerged as "the sole expression of Arab nationalism in Damascus." It overwhelmed the communists, the Muslim Brotherhood, and the old political parties. Michel Aflaq, then a schoolteacher and a writer of note, gave the party its "necessary romanticism." In the Damascus of his time, Aflaq stood out: he read Friedrich Nietzsche and Andre Gide, and he explicated Marcel Proust and Thomas Mann. He was more of an artist than a politician, disconnected from the life of "the herd," and lived in his own world. A handful of young men made up the initial membership. They were secondary school graduates recruited by their teachers. The party had drawn five hundred members by 1952. "Party work consumed us, we devoted our labor and entire lives to it. Were I to give examples of personal sacrifice I would need to compose many books." No village was too remote for the young Baathists. There were villagers who had never seen a physician before, and the Baathist physicians called on these forlorn peasants and treated them for free.

At first, the peasants had not accepted these young rebels. "They considered us a threat to their sacred beliefs, but our stubbornness drew us closer to them." Agrarian society was riddled with oppression, and this had given the Baath its foothold. The success of the party in the countryside was made easier by the rural origins of the young cadres: though they were university students in Damascus, they hailed from the same countryside they were trying to convert to their cause. Damascus did not yield to the Baath, Jundi writes. The party was looking for quick results, and political work in Damascus was hard and demanding. Of Damascus, Jundi writes: "It is the city of Arab history, it does not submit except to a lover worthy of its seduction. It is the city of waiting, it takes its time, it hesitates, then it either says no or it accepts. Its refusal means that it is impossible to go on, its acceptance signifies entering history through the widest of gates. Islam founded a great state only after Damascus raised its banners. In the same vein, pan-Arabism would not have become an ideology of consequence had Damascus not taken to it." The Baath had not studied and mastered those age-old ways of Damascus. Terror was to close the gap between the party and the great, bewildering city.

Political prisons would become the distinct mark of Syrian political life. The notorious Mezze prison would now stalk the political world. In their innocence, Jundi recalls, the Baathists had boasted that they would turn this prison into a tourist hotel and put an end to prisons and torture. The reverse had happened in a whirlwind of violence. "Henceforth, the Syrian citizen would open his ears and heart every morning to the expectation that he would hear martial music, and the announcement of Military Communiqué Number 1." The heroes of yesterday would become today's villains. The Baath had neutralized other parties, but it was consumed by schisms within. Officers and ideologues dueled within the Baath. It was important to them that they outdo the celebrated Egyptian Gamal Abdel Nasser and show up his "socialism" with a more drastic economic program. The younger generation warred against the elders. "We reached power after all the other forces had been defeated, we fulfilled the desires of imperialism as we shouted against it." This was the era of endless purges: hundreds of officers were sacked, and the nation's army became dueling cabals. The ideologues had spoken of the competing "wings" in the Baath Party, but these were warring "tribes," Jundi bitterly notes. "The hands of the Baathists were now sullied with blood and shame, with the Baathists outdoing each other in killings and oppression."

Hafez al-Assad turned out to be both the exemplar and beneficiary of this time of radical rupture. He rode it to power, he was a better conspirator than the rest, and he could at the same time promise a stern soldier's peace, an antidote to the chaos. Before his vaunted "corrective" coup d'état, he was dueling Salah Jadid, a fellow Alawite officer, and Nur al-Din al-Atasi, a physician and Sunni head of state. Atasi was in truth a cover for the Alawi commanders. It was winner-take-all in this unforgiving game. Assad would secure his reign, and the other two men would be dispatched to the Mezze prison. Atasi would remain there until his release in 1992, when he was sent on a stretcher to Paris, to expire of cancer. Jadid's end would come a year later in the wretched Mezze prison.

It was fortunate for Sami al-Jundi that he was a skilled dentist and that he hadn't risen so high that he had to pay a terrible price. He would know exile—the saving graces of dentistry in Tunisia and the crafting of memoirs. Syria now belonged to its new master. He would reshape it in his own image—secretive, drab, and cunning, a republic of fear and shadows. In 1971, one year after

Assad's rise to power, he was to give Hamud al-Shufi, a Baath
Party leader who was to break with him in later years, the crux of
his view of politics and of man. People have "primarily economic
demands," he said, such things as acquiring a plot of land, a car,
a house, etc. Those demands could be met, he said, in "one way
or another." But there were individuals, "one or two hundred" at
most, who were political men, and those were destined to oppose
him no matter what. "It is for them that the Mezze prison was
originally intended."

This sentiment was no doubt a window into the mind of this
most consequential of Syria's leaders in modern times. What
would prove to be at variance with the truth were the numbers
who would be dispatched to political prisons. Thousands would
be relegated to that fate. It didn't take much dissent to land in
Syria's cruel prisons—a wrong word uttered in public, a rumor,
an association with an outlawed political group, a discussion that
would hint at the ruler's Alawi background. Men had to abandon
politics to survive. One haunting case chronicled by the acclaimed
dissident writer Ahmad Faraj Birqdar, who had spent nearly 15
years in prison, was about a man known as Mazen Abu al-Hilm.
Mazen is sent to prison for a dream he had had. Mazen tells
Birqdar that the dream was obscure and jumbled, that it had a
funeral of a high official, perhaps a military coup d'état. Mazen
had not confessed to the dream. But a close friend of his had been
arrested and tortured, and Mazen's name had come up during the
torture sessions. The friend had not been able to bear the torture
and had told of Mazen's dream, and Mazen had been arrested.
He had had no political affiliations, but the dream was taken as
evidence of hostility to the regime, and the man had landed in
prison. It was the "most costly dream in the world," a fellow
inmate said.

Birqdar, who was born in Homs in 1951 and was a recipient of the PEN/Barbara Goldsmith Freedom to Write Award in 1999 and a Hellman/Hammett Free Expression prize a year later, was to go through all of his country's dreaded prisons: Mezze, the desert prison in Palmyra, Saydnaya military prison. He was to be held for years without any charges filed against him. Released in November 2000 by presidential amnesty—in the first year of Bashar's reign—he left the country never to return. A memoir of that cruel time, *The Betrayals of Language and Silence*, which was published in Beirut in 2006, is a testament to free spirit that endured hell but was never broken. Birqdar, a communist activist, was the third in his immediate family to be imprisoned; his wife was to endure the same punishment. His only daughter was three years old when he entered prison; he was released when she was about to start her university education. For six of those years of imprisonment, he had been cut off from the outside world, denied visits, pen and paper, access to radio broadcasts. He had been an accomplished poet, and the most searing part of this spare prison narrative has his daughter now allowed to see this virtual stranger, prisoner number 13. His fellow prisoners scramble to get him the right clothing for the occasion, and he recognizes his shy daughter, half-concealed by his mother. On a subsequent visit, the daughter asks, "Father, is it true that you are a poet?" "Almost," he answers. "Why then don't you write a poem for me?" He had written many poems for her, he says, and she will read them in the fullness of time, when she grows up. "I don't want them later, I want you to write for me now." He composes a poem for her, full of associations and hints that may speak to her. She embraces him on the next visit. "Father, I memorized it," she says. She looks around in fear when he asks her to recite the poem for him, and declines. This was life in prison, the "kingdom of death and madness." Pens were made out of splinters of wood, ink out of tea and onionskin. Amid the humiliation, the hunger, and the torture sessions, the prisoners, Birqdar recalls, grew enamored of their cells, returned to them as one returns to the safety of the womb.

It was part of the hagiography of Hafez al-Assad that he had opened up Syria's prisons when he came to power and that he reined in the madness of the preceding decades. It was recalled that the adoring crowds in Aleppo had lifted his car off the ground when he visited in the first year of his presidency. Syrians were comforted then by his steadiness and restraint. But this was apologetics; it is true he was not a sadist in his resort to violence— for there was method to his cruelty, and a calm and deliberateness to the man himself. Interlocutors who dealt with him say that he never raised his voice and that he was not one for bluster and empty threats. He was, at best, a mediocre public speaker. There was little if any visible fire or zeal in him. (In his first decade at the helm, he had farmed out the cruelty to his younger brother Rifaat, who had not recoiled from violence and personal depravity.) He built a polity in his own image, and he did it patiently, with guile and cruelty applied in equal measure. He had built it against the background of the Cold War, in the mold of the dictatorships of Eastern Europe and the Communist bloc. There had been tumult, conspiracies, and military seizures of power in Syria's history after independence; he brought that to an end. In the national security state of this military ruler, the son informed on his family, the wife betrayed the secrets of her husband. Tens of thousands were dispatched to political prisons, and the system of terror set across the entire country, from the principal cities to the remotest villages.

"Do we lie now when we say that the life of the slaves of Rome reenacts itself in Syria, but only in a twentieth-century form?" Birqdar said in a memorable defense before the state's highest military court in 1993. This was a quarter-century after Jundi's memoirs, and this writer had endured years in prison with yet more to come. It had been hell in captivity, he said, and "we dragged our chains along into this court." A regime that had itself come to power through force and conspiracy can't prosecute any citizen for his opinion, regardless of whether he "was a socialist or a capitalist, a believer or an atheist, a supporter of the regime, or an opponent." Birqadr spoke of the capriciousness of political life: "No one would quarrel with the proposition that had this regime that came to power through a military coup in 1970 failed in its bid, your court now would be trying the coup leaders on charges of being enemies of the state and the party." There were no rules and no laws in this republic. There was only the law of pure might and force, so much so that one can't "see any difference between the word Syria and the word surrealistic." This court has no standing independent of the regime, Birqdar said, and its proceedings are a pure charade, an adornment of the dictatorship and its absolute power. "I testify and affirm that future generations in Syria will bow their heads in shame when they stop and ponder these black pages in our history. Who tries whom? I want to thank my mother who taught me that freedom is mightier than our prisons."

The trail of unrestrained violence, which had opened up in the early 1960s, had not been shaken off. There was silence in the land, and the prisons were crowded. In Birqdar's chronicle, a political prisoner with a clever turn of phrase laments a country that can't build enough prisons for its people. And there were the killings. No one has come forth with a reliable estimate of those who had been killed by the regime.

It was the mark of the despotism that its mercilessness at home was covered up by its "success" at the game of states. Hafez al-Assad broke his country, and his Alawite background had fed and propelled the terror. He was the son of peasantry, a schismatic in the quintessential country of Sunni Islam. Damascus had been the seat of the Umayyad dynasty (661–750), the repository of orthodox, urban Islam's truth. This was where Islam made its first stand when it spilled beyond the Arabian Peninsula, which mattered to Syria's self-image. There were minorities, no fewer than 18 sects, and ethnic communities, but pride of place belonged to the principal cities—Aleppo, Damascus, Homs, Hama—and to the Sunni faith that dominated these cities.

The order of merchants, urban notables, and bureaucratic families took its hegemony for granted. It never occurred to the Sunnis that an Alawite soldier who hailed from the peasantry would come to rule the proud, tumultuous cities. Hafez al-Assad tread carefully. His ascent to power, beginning in the late 1960s, was cautious in the extreme. He hid behind Sunni frontmen and did his best to reassure the great merchant families and houses that their interests would be protected by his regime, that he was a safe bet against more radical ideologies in the Baath Party and the military. Always conscious of the affront that his Alawi background presented to the more conservative and diehards among the Sunnis, he obtained a fatwa from an ally in Lebanon, Imam Musa al-Sadr, that the Alawis were a community of mainstream Shiites. Sadr, the Iranian-born activist cleric, had come to Lebanon in 1959 and rose steadily in the political world of Beirut and beyond. This wasn't a perfect solution—because a hidebound Sunni shopkeeper or artisan in Homs and Hama viewed Shiites with a jaundiced eye—but it was the best the military ruler could do. By the strict canons of mainstream (Sunni) Islam, Shiism wasn't quite the heresy that the Alawi faith was thought to be. Alert to his community's isolation, Hafez al-Assad tried to push it into the religious mainstream. The veneration of the Prophet's son-in-law, Imam Ali, so central to the Alawite faith, was reined in, and the ruler himself did his best to seem at one with Sunni practice: he prayed in public, broke his fast during the month of Ramadan in the company of religious scholars, and displayed the piety expected of a man who had come into dominion in a city so central to Islam as Damascus. In the course of his presidency, five mosques would be built in his ancestral (Alawite) village, the largest named for the ruler's mother.

It hadn't been easy for him to secure the acceptance of his country. As the dictatorship tightened its hold in the course of the 1970s, Hafez al-Assad bent the Sunni religious institution to his will. He gave the clerics leeway and deference but limited their political role. Sunni jurisprudence stressed obedience to the ruler, the avoidance of *fitna* (sedition), and the Sunni jurists appointed by the state had lived by that code. The temper of the official religious establishment was defined by a man of the clerical guild who had been appointed grand mufti of the republic in 1964, Ahmad Kuftaro (1915–2004). Kuftaro, who stayed at the helm for four decades, had risen to his position through political patronage—he had not been favored by his peers in the religious class. In 1971, in a stark violation of precedent, he had accepted an appointment to the parliament. He would give the regime and its Alawi master the cover and the support they needed. In 1991, he gave the routine reelection of Hafez al-Assad an unusual warrant, describing it as "a national obligation and religious duty." Caution and subtlety had paid off for the ruler, and in that era of politico-religious disputation, Hafez al-Assad was lucky in the enemies he drew. His rule was contested by the Muslim Brotherhood, and its radicalization would become a prop of the regime. It was better to have a ruler who was merciless but predictable, than a politico-religious movement that was a menace to public order and stability. He struck a bargain with the Damascus (Sunni) merchant class. He would rein in the ideologues and let the *souk* be. In return, the merchants would extend him their support. And the bargain held through his rule.

Hafez al-Assad delighted in describing himself as a "peasant" and the son of a peasant. To a meeting of the Peasants General Union, he spoke with nostalgia for his village roots. "I had a passion for threshing the harvest, but I took part in all phases of farming, lived your emotions, and understand your sentiments." This was 1980 and he had been at the apex of power for a full decade; he was grieving for a past he had been determined to escape. "Fellow peasants," he was to say to the same association a year later, "no hand will after this day be above your hand. . . . You are the producers. Yours is the power." The Baath Party was avowedly socialist, and in the fashion of the time, "agrarian reform" was a pillar of its ideology. This was the perfect vehicle for Alawis coming into their own and assaulting the old order of property, social standing, and political power. The peasantry didn't wield power, but they were a shield of the regime and a loyal base of support. The countryside was mobilized as a counter to the traditional primacy of the cities.

Hafez al-Assad's great test—and the test of his Alawi community for that matter—came a decade into his rule in the form of an insurrection that lasted three years (1979–1982) and played out in the two cities of Aleppo and Hama. The mask of the regime had fallen, and the patience of the Sunni urbanites had worn thin. This bloody tale has been repeatedly told—in the public mind indentified with Hama and the cruelty inflicted on it by the regime in February 1982. But the insurrection also had broken out in the larger northern city of Aleppo. If a single incident can

be said to have ignited this merciless fight, it was an assault on
June 16, 1979, against Alawi cadets at the artillery school. An
army captain—a Sunni with no known links to the Muslim
Brotherhood who, on the surface, was a Baathist tasked with
indoctrinating the cadets—had pulled off a horrific attack. He
had separated the Alawis (out of 300 cadets enrolled in that academy, 282 were Alawis) and machine-gunned 83 of them. There
were subsequent attacks on Baath Party offices, and before long
Aleppo had become a theatre of war, the souk had emerged as a
battleground, and the mosques were pressed into the fight. The
Muslim Brotherhood now provided the troops of this insurgency.

Nothing was off-limits in this war for both the security forces
and the Aleppines determined to be done with this regime. In
this old trading city, the regime's forces were strangers, an occupation force for all intents and purposes. The ruling Baath Party
hardly figured here, a cadre of 600 members in a city of 1 million
people. The Aleppine troubles had borne out a minority sentiment among the Alawis, the anxiety of a long-persecuted community that the sins of the regime would become Alawi sins by
association. French sociologist Michel Seurat wrote at the time
that Alawi parents of the murdered cadets had refused to receive
the condolences of the officials who called on them. But the ruler
rallied his community and successfully linked its survival with that
of his regime. An assassination attempt on Assad in June 1980
let loose draconian terror. The ruler's younger brother Rifaat, the
guardian of the regime and the commander of its *Saraya al-Difaa*
(Defense Companies), declared all-out war against the Muslim
Brotherhood and those who stood by it. In a widely circulated
statement, he declared that the regime was ready to kill a million
Syrians in order to defend "the revolution." A defining act of
cruelty gave this fight a terrible marker: one day after the assassination attempt on Hafez al-Assad, attack helicopters sent to the

Palmyra desert prison gunned down 800 political prisoners in one bloody spree.

The regime wanted this barbarism known. The Palmyra killings were a prelude to the mass slaughter in Hama. This ruler was there to stay, and he let the violence and his brother deliver his central message. The demonstrations of old—the street protests, the jacqueries in Hama, where petty fights would break out between Alawi villagers and the prickly city folk—were a thing of the past.

After this time of terror, all restraints were pushed aside as the regime's functionaries set out to embellish the cult of Hafez al-Assad and give it that suffocating presence in public life. The Baath Party now receded into the background, and the ruler assumed the center of the political iconography. This was a cult with a heavy rural touch. The dictator's mother, an old peasant woman, became the nation's mother, and her death in 1992 was turned into a national day of grief. There were murals and portraits of her with her headcover, looking over her son. This had been forced onto an urban population with a legendary contempt for peasants. Trendy young people all over the Levant fled at the sight of relatives who looked like Naaisa al-Assad, pretending they had no connection to them. But in her son's republic, the pretense had to be kept up. Then there was the cult of the oldest son after his death in a car accident two years later. Basel was "the engineer," "the knight," the repository of a nation's hopes snatched away by a cruel death. The regime, its social base, and its Alawi core can be said to have "ruralized" Damascus. Physically, the countryside was spilling into the city, but there was also cultural change—the conquest of power by the peasantry.

A sophisticated Lebanese journalist with an eye for the social history of Syria, Jihad al-Zeine gave the country's agony in 2011, and the Sunni-Alawi split, an essential grounding in the struggle between the urban elites and the forces of the countryside. In his telling, the history of the past century telescopes easily from the end of the Great War, the collapse of Ottoman authority, to the present. From 1920 until 1958, the urban elites and their base in the four principal cities of Damascus, Aleppo, Homs, and Hama were ascendant. There was an interregnum between 1958 and 1963, and then came the triumph of the boys of the hinterland and of the military. In their time of primacy, the urban (Sunni) elites had shown scant concern for the rural population, and they took their dominion for granted. By 1958, their world was collapsing and radical ideological movements were knocking at the gates. These elites sought an escape in a union with Egypt's Gamal Abdel Nasser. That merger, the United Arab Republic, had been doomed from the start: the Syrian elites were quarrelsome, the Egyptians overbearing. The experiment ended in acrimony and several years of drift in the politics of Syria. Radical Baathists from the military and Alawis, Druze, and Ismailis from the countryside now claimed power. They were "socialists," they proclaimed, and their program had a heavy dose of class and sectarian revenge. A man from their midst, Hafez al-Assad, had proved both lucky and a cunning political player. Where so many of his peers, contemporaries, and rivals fell to assassins' bullets or perished in prison, he was to rule for three decades, die a natural death, and be buried in his ancestral (Alawi) village. More remarkable still, he was able to change the tumultuous polity into a regime of republican dynasticism. This was the regime that the protesters sought to topple when the Arab Spring tantalized and excited the Syrians.

If the urban elites had been arrogant and indifferent to the needs of the rural population, the new men in power were given to despotism and cruelty. Doubtless, they always felt the burden of their old disinheritance and they were under no illusions about how the old bourgeois classes viewed them. As the new men of the countryside leveled the old order, they pined for its privileges. They moved to Damascus, married into the most exalted families of Damascus and Homs, put on airs, and grew phenomenally wealthy. By the time their country erupted against them, they had come into control of the military-security establishment, the economy, the religious institution, and a system of propaganda that spread the cult of the Assads, father and son. There were shades of North Korea in this Syrian regime. There were estimates of 3,000 statues of the Old Man by the time of his death. A primitive cult of personality robbed the country of whatever political vitality it once had.

CHAPTER FOUR

False Dawn

B ASHAR'S "COMING OUT," his debut on the diplomatic stage, was to take place in February 2005, and a political murder in Lebanon was to batter the wall of secrecy around him. In retrospect, the February 14 assassination of Lebanon's former Prime Minister Rafik Hariri in a car bombing on Beirut's seafront would become Bashar's defining deed, his stepping out of his father's shadow. The father had ordered his share of killings in Lebanon, but this murder would be different. Like with the murder of King Duncan in *Macbeth*, the perpetrators here didn't know that their victim had so much blood. The assassination of this preeminent Sunni leader who had clashed with Damascus over the terms of his country's freedom of maneuver in the face of Syria's hegemony would haunt Bashar and his regime. In truth, Hariri was the unlikeliest of martyrs for the cause of Lebanon's independence. He had risen from the obscurity and poverty of Sidon—on Lebanon's coast—to the upper reaches of Lebanese and Arab society, largely through the patronage of the House of Saud and the inner dealings of Arab rulers and courtiers. He wasn't particularly articulate or given to the call of political causes. He believed in the power of wealth and pragmatism, and he saw Lebanon's mission in the time-honored way of Sidon's Phoenician heritage: commerce and trade, banking and tourism. Over two long decades in the political game, he had made his accommodation with Syrian power. He paid off Syrian intelligence operatives and officers, cut their sons and daughters and wives into business deals, handed out cash when called upon to do so by the Syrian intelligence barons, and did what he could for the restoration of his country, all while staying on the safe side of Syria's power in Lebanon.

Hariri knew the risks of Syria's wrath: for three decades, bigger players than he had been struck down right when they had begun to agitate for their country's sovereignty against the power of Damascus. In 1977, it had been the turn of a Druze leader by the name of Kamal Jumblatt. He was assassinated because he was a proud and difficult man of Mount Lebanon who had paid no heed to Syria's claims of hegemony. Five years later, it had been a headstrong young Maronite, Bashir Gemayel, who had risen through the civil war of Lebanon to the heights of power. Gemayel had been elected president in the cruel summer of 1982, when Israel invaded Lebanon to destroy the armed Palestinian movement. He was a Lebanese nationalist, eager to put together a state that had come apart. But he was never to assume office. In a memorable deed of terror, a blast shattered the three-story building of his political party's headquarters and took his life. There would be other victims along the way—a president, a prime minister, lesser political figures. The regime in Damascus was hell-bent on erasing the border between Syria and Lebanon.

"Beirut is a city of tactics," U.S. Secretary of State George P. Shultz wrote in his memoirs, *Turmoil and Triumph* (1993). He had been embroiled in the politics of Lebanon in 1982–84, when he had tried to secure for the Lebanese a margin of maneuver in relation to Syria. The noble effort had not worked. The Lebanese political class was its fractured self and frightened in the extreme. Its fate was to go up against a master strategist in Damascus, the ruler Hafez al-Assad. Methodically—patience was the man's trademark—he had driven out or marginalized other outside players in Lebanon, and all he left the Lebanese was the shell of national sovereignty.

The Syrian political and military class around Hafez al-Assad would come to believe that Lebanon was its rightful claim. The Lebanese had been careless. They had feuded among themselves, and the Syrians had ridden those jealousies—and the pretext of an Israeli military presence in southern Lebanon—into veritable acquisition of their smaller neighbor. Lebanon was now ruled from Anjar, a hitherto inconsequential town close to the Syrian border. It was in Anjar that Syria's military and intelligence commissars held court.

A great, pitiless hoax was played on Lebanon. A country that had known the crosscurrents of the world, a place of culture—French culture in east Beirut and Mount Lebanon, American culture on the western seaboard—was to pass into the control of the conquering army of a brutal, backward regime. The Syrians had uses for Lebanon: there was money there for the Syrian kleptocracy, opportunities for drug dealings and contraband, and a border from which the Syrians could wage intermittent wars and deeds of terror against Israel while maintaining the most quiet of borders on the Syrian-Israeli front.

Truth be known, this steady encroachment on Lebanon was aided and abetted by the silence of the world. In one of those astonishing changes, the Syrian arsonists had come to be seen as the fire brigade of a volatile Lebanese polity. The Lebanese were given to a belief that their country mattered to the United States. But the Pax Americana had averted its gaze from the Syrian destruction of the last vestige of Lebanon's independence. In 1990–91, the United States had acquiesced when the Syrians put down the rebellion of a Lebanese officer, Michel Aoun, who had dared to defy Syrian writ in his country. This was the price paid by President George Herbert Walker Bush for enlisting Syria in the coalition that waged war against Saddam Hussein for his grab of Kuwait. Pity the Lebanese: they had cedars, Kuwait had oil. Kuwait's sovereignty would be restored while the Lebanese were consigned to their terrible fate in that big Syrian prison. Hariri was struck down as he had set out to find his own way, away from Syria's embrace. He had been bullied by the Syrians some months before his assassination. On the face of it, Hariri's wealth, ties to the House of Saud, and close friendship with French President Jacques Chirac gave him a measure of protection. But Bashar al-Assad was a brittle man determined to demonstrate his own authority.

Hariri's assassination was the chronicle of a death foretold. The countdown to his murder began some five months earlier. The two decades of political traffic between Hariri and Hafez al-Assad were of little consequence now. Bashar al-Assad made no secret of his aversion to Hariri. Doubtless, the stature of Rafik Hariri, a Sunni politician with wide horizons and contacts the world over, was unsettling to Mr. Assad and the cabal around him. Bashar had sought and secured the extension of the mandate of his satrap in Lebanon, President Emile Lahoud, a bitter foe of Hariri. This was something of a violation of the constitutional practice of Lebanon, because the president was limited to six years in office. The affair hadn't been pretty or smooth. Hariri, who had been prime minister for ten of the preceding twelve years, was summoned to Damascus. The chronology is of some importance here: a meeting with President Assad took place August 24, 2004. Gone were the niceties, the storytelling, and the drawn-out meetings that Assad Senior was known for. This meeting was to last ten to fifteen minutes. (Fourteen minutes was the exact number given by Hariri himself.)

Rafik Hariri was brusquely informed that the extension of Lahoud's mandate would take place because such was Bashar's will and decision. The Syrian warned that he would "break Lebanon" over the heads of Hariri and Walid Jumblatt, the preeminent leader among the Druze and a noted figure in the opposition to Syria's hegemony. As Hariri told the story of his meeting to several interlocutors upon his return to Beirut, there had been no diplomatic finesse. Bashar had warned him that the Syrians would find him and his family "anywhere in the world." Hariri was not to be comforted, Bashar said, by his close ties to the French president, for if "Chirac puts me out of Lebanon, I will consider different options and will let you know." The Syrians had long emptied Lebanon of any meaningful sense of sovereignty, and Bashar left no ambiguity in this regard. "I am personally interested in this matter. It is not about Emile Lahoud, but about Bashar al-Assad." Bashar, the young eye doctor, had come into his own sense of political mastery. This was not quite the way his father would have done it, but Syria was Bashar's polity now.

Hariri knew he would be a marked man if he defied Bashar's wishes. He hedged his bets, submitted his resignation, voted in parliament for Lahoud's extension, and let the word out that he was probing his political options. His government was replaced by one of quislings. A quiescent Sunni politician from the city of Tripoli headed a new cabinet. The relative legitimacy that had been accorded Hariri's cabinet was denied the successor government. Bashar al-Assad now faced the prospect of Hariri, the leading figure of his community, bringing his followers and international standing into the gathering opposition to Syria's occupation.

It was in the midst of this crisis that the United Nations Security Council adopted Resolution 1559, sponsored by France and the United States, calling for a "free and fair electoral process in Lebanon's upcoming presidential election . . . without foreign interference" and for "all remaining foreign forces to withdraw from Lebanon." The timing was telling: the U.N. Security Council vote took place September 2, and the hapless Lebanese parliament was to rubber-stamp the extension of Lahoud's tenure a day later.

There was no way Hariri could convince the ruling cabal in Damascus that he had not been the godfather of that Security Council Resolution. He pleaded his case with a seasoned and sly operative of the Syrian regime, Deputy Foreign Minister Walid al-Moallem. In this meeting, Hariri was his conciliatory self. He was a friend of Syria, he would insist, but he wanted an end to the plots and bullying against him. Syria's operatives in Lebanon—the intelligence officers and the Lebanese security services that answered to Damascus—had been hounding him, but he was not a French, European, or American agent, he said. He wanted Lebanon's ties to Syria preserved, but the world had changed and Lebanon could not be governed from Damascus. He knew Jacques Chirac, but Chirac had been "as reliable as a watch for nine years" and had been of service to Syria itself. In his own defense, Hariri said he knew that he was dealing with a "young president" in Damascus, and that were he to clash with Bashar, there would be terrible consequences for him and for Lebanon as well. It was his hope that his fidelity to Syria over the course of 25 years would spare him Damascus's wrath. He had the votes in parliament to block the extension of Lahoud, but he understood that this would be seen as a personal failure of Bashar, and hence he had given that extension his vote and that of his parliamentary coalition. Moallem was an old hand, Hariri was twisting in the wind. He would be shown no sympathy. "We have cornered you," Moallem said, and he was speaking both for the Damascus regime and its collaborators in Beirut.

Bashar had defied the mighty Franco-American alliance. But the Syrian regime could not rest easy. The Lebanese had grown emboldened, and their sovereignty suddenly mattered to the outside world. The assassination of Hariri had backfired. Lebanese of all stripes now had a martyr in Rafik Hariri. Those who had mocked "tycoonism" and dismissed him as a tool of Saudi Arabia embraced his cult. The Sunnis of Lebanon who had been quiescent and uncertain of their place in the country stirred to life. The ghost of Hariri, it is fair to say, was to prove mightier than the man. His political heirs were skilled in the way they worked the victim's cult. In the Lebanese dynastic fashion, Hariri's son, Saad, became the standard-bearer of the Hariri cause. The family owned a television station, Future TV, and it saturated the airwaves with moving tributes to the man, his love of country, and his dreams for it. In death, Rafik Hariri had become an inspiration to the Sunnis and an ecumenical figure of modernity and philanthropy. This was not lost on the Syrian rulers. They had done their best to intimidate the Lebanese, and now the Hariri cult blew at will and had a resonance among the Sunnis in Syria itself. Hariri had been devout, but in moderation. He remained, in his presentation of self, a boy of the town of Sidon who had done well, the perfect Sunni bourgeois. He had scaled the heights but was deferential to the religious establishment. He found—and funded—moderate Sunni clerics and spent liberally on them and their projects. No one could accuse him of extremism. He was an enemy of the jihadist enterprise and thus gave the Sunnis a decent political alternative. Strictly speaking, his arena was

Lebanon, but a brittle, minoritarian regime in Damascus couldn't be sure of that.

An extortion racket that had been immensely lucrative to the barons of the Syrian regime was threatened: it had grown both cruel and complacent, it had (rightly) assumed that the world had wearied of the Lebanese and that Syria's writ over that country was seen as the best of a bad lot. In an exquisite historical twist, on February 2, 2005, in his State of the Union address, President George W. Bush would undo the policy that his own father had accepted and would announce a radically different American approach. "Syria still allows its territory, and parts of Lebanon, to be used by terrorists who seek to destroy every chance of peace in the region. You have passed and we are applying the Syrian Accountability Act, and we expect the Syrian government to end all support for terror and open the door to freedom." The Syrian Accountability and Lebanese Sovereignty Restoration Act, a congressional initiative of 2003, had given the president broad authority to impose a range of economic sanctions and restrictions on Syria. Hitherto, the White House had treated that initiative with considerable reserve, so its embrace signaled a change in Washington. American power was nearby on Syria's eastern border, in Iraq. A Baathist tyranny in Baghdad had been demolished, and there were "neocons"—a veritable obsession of the Syrian regime—in Washington speaking of "low-hanging fruit" and of retribution against regimes that harbor terror. There was paranoia to spare in Arab political circles about a new American imperial bid to remake the Arab world, and that paranoia was particularly severe in Damascus.

This must have been the time the regime in Damascus and its allies in the Hezbollah movement in Beirut made the decision to murder Rafik Hariri. There had been a guessing game as to whether the assassins would come for Hariri or his ally, Walid Jumblatt. The Druze leader had a powerful community of Druze in Syria, and his father had been struck down by the Syrians in 1977. Hariri was the target this time. Four days before the explosion that took his life and the lives of 22 other people, a savvy Norwegian diplomat, UN Special Envoy Terje Roed-Larsen, had warned Hariri. The Norwegian, who had made a trip to Damascus, said there was a "very high risk for violence and assassinations" and that Hariri had better tread carefully. A similar warning was given him by French President Chirac. It had all been to no avail.

The meaning of this assassination was not lost on the Syrian reformers and intellectual class. No one yet had incontrovertible evidence on the identity of the killers, but the trail from the crime scene in Beirut led to Damascus. A big crime had taken place, and it was assumed that it could not have been done without a green light from the pinnacle of power in Damascus. Hariri's son and political inheritor, Saad, noted that he did not hear from Bashar, that no condolences had come from the Syrian ruler. But an "open letter" of condolences from a group of prominent Syrian thinkers and oppositionists was published in Lebanon's most trusted daily, *An-Nahar*, on February 24. This murder, the letter read, was a "terrible, ugly deed of slaughter planned and perpetrated by those who do not wish to see Lebanon healthy, united, and free. We fully support your demand for the withdrawal of the Syrian army from Lebanon, for the rectification of Syrian-Lebanese relations, for the building of a relationship based on equality, independence, and the free choice of both peoples. We have long expressed this view through means available to us, for we as educated Syrians have found in Lebanon a window for the expression of ideas not permitted us in our own homeland."

If there were Syrians curious about the young inheritor now in the saddle in their country, this murder in Beirut confirmed their worst fears. The regime had not changed, Bashar was his father's son. The killing machine was not done. Four months after Hariri's assassination, on June 2, a car bomb killed a flamboyant, heedlessly anti-Syrian commentator for *An-Nahar* newspaper, Samir Kassir. Where Hariri had been cautious, Kassir tempted fate. His enmity toward the Syrian military presence in Lebanon was absolute and undisguised. Forty-five years of age, Kassir embodied the open ways of Beirut. He was Greek Orthodox, his mother a 1948 Palestinian refugee, his father a Syrian. He straddled the fence between journalism and academia, moving back and forth between his work at *An-Nahar* and a teaching appointment at Saint Joseph University in east Beirut. He paid tribute to the city in a sprawling history of it, *Histoire de Beyrouth*. The book had been published in Paris two years before his murder. He chronicled the city from its early beginnings to the "end of its innocence," and its descent into political troubles. Kassir's devotion suffuses the book, all the more so because the city had given refuge to his parents. Beirut reciprocated and gave him a moving farewell. Two thousand people carried his coffin from the *An-Nahar* offices through Martyrs' Square, the city's center, to a nearby church. His colleague and editor-in-chief Gebran Tueni, three years his elder, was an equally passionate critic of the Syrian policy in Lebanon. Tueni minced no words. The perpetrators were Syrians, he said, "they are responsible from head to toe. Bashar al-Assad should not be allowed to have a single intelligence operative in Lebanon."

Reality outstripped fiction in the Beirut inferno. Six months later, on December 12, eighty-eight pounds of TNT packed in a car was triggered by remote control. The explosion blew Gebran

Tueni's sport-utility vehicle over the side of a hill, killing him and two others. Tueni was heir to a publishing dynasty in a Greek Orthodox family. His grandfather and namesake had launched *An-Nahar* in 1933; his father, Ghassan, was a legendary publisher and political figure who at one time or another had a seat in the country's parliament, represented Lebanon at the United Nations, and opined on the issues faced by his country. Ghassan's son had inherited his father's gift for writing, but the doings of Lebanon, now in Syria's shadow, had been altered. "The Syrian regime didn't offer anything to Syria, didn't offer anything to Lebanon," Gebran Tueni had said in an interview two months before his assassination. "This regime lives on mafias, lives on money laundering, lives on drug dealing, lives on corruption." He knew he was in harm's way, so he left for Paris and stayed there a few months. He was struck down the day after his return.

Bashar al-Assad was as good as his word. He had warned Hariri that were he to be pushed out of Lebanon he would consider his alternatives. Syria's foes were falling to car bombs and assassins. Bashar's army had been forced out of Lebanon, but his intelligence operatives and the Lebanese he had empowered and sustained were busy hacking away at the fragile independence the Lebanese had secured. Tueni was without doubt the intellectual leader of the opposition. A diplomatic cable from Damascus had it right: "This was a message to the Lebanese opposition, we are still here despite all the pressure, and can reach you; your new friends can't protect you." Bashar and his cabal were in no mood to accept the loss of their lucrative dominion in Lebanon. The Lebanese had handed Hariri's political heirs a sweeping victory in a parliamentary election, but the Syrians were determined to overturn it. They had a case of seller's remorse; they had quit Lebanon under duress and were eager to retrieve what they had given up.

In the aftermath of the withdrawal from Lebanon, there was speculation that the retreat would spill into Syria and that the regime's hold on power at home would give way. But this was not to be. The dictatorship rode out that setback, grew increasingly repressive, and set out to make its way back into Lebanon and to do all it could to frustrate America in Iraq. Truth be told, the "Cedar Revolution" had given the Lebanese liberty, a child of George W. Bush's "diplomacy of freedom." In his memoirs, *Decision Points*, Mr. Bush rightly claimed that revolt as "one of the most important successes of the freedom agenda." That challenge to Syria had come early in Bush's second term, but before long the Bush diplomacy would falter. A year after Hariri's assassination there was renewed swagger in Damascus. A crisis far away in Denmark, the publication of cartoons depicting the Prophet Muhammad, gave the regime room to maneuver, an opportunity for it to pose as a defender of Islam in orchestrated riots. The red carpet was rolled out for Iranian President Mahmoud Ahmadinejad, a reminder to the United States that Damascus still had diplomatic options. Bashar was now convinced that he could outwait the Bush administration, and defy and thwart it in Lebanon. An election in the West Bank and Gaza went Hamas's way, and in November 2006 American voters gave the Democratic Party a resounding victory in the congressional elections. The faith in America's prowess was receding, and all George W. Bush could concentrate on was the rescue of the American war in Iraq. The "surge" he opted for came in the nick of time. The American position in Iraq and the new Iraqi order were salvaged. The Sunnis of Iraq had turned against Al Qaeda, so decisive had their defeat turned out to be at the hands of the Shia militias. There was little left in the American arsenal, and Lebanon would have to fend for itself against the reassertion of Syrian power.

By the time 2006 had drawn to a close, the balance of power within the Bush administration had shifted. Secretary of Defense Donald Rumsfeld would be replaced by a more conventional player, Robert Gates. The power of Vice President Dick Cheney had eroded, and George W. Bush was winding down his presidency. In November 2007, with one year left on its watch, the Bush administration had convened a diplomatic conference in Annapolis, Maryland, yet another grand diplomatic gathering meant to address the Israeli-Palestinian conflict. The Syrians were there in Annapolis, and hence back in contention. This sort of diplomacy was their stock-in-trade. They had behind them more than three decades of experience at drawn-out Arab-Israeli meetings mediated by the Americans. Things were breaking their way. A nasty war in the summer of 2006 between Hezbollah and Israel, triggered by Hezbollah's abduction of two Israeli soldiers, had given that militia prestige and a greater freedom to maneuver within Lebanon. The axis of Iran, Syria, and Hezbollah had withstood a period of American assertiveness. America's allies in Lebanon were thrown on the defensive. The dreaded "neocons" in Washington had had their moment.

The Cedar Revolution had been heady. Its choreography was nothing short of dazzling, with young people in Beirut's plazas displaying love of country and defiance of their Syrian tormentors. Hariri's son, Saad, had been a darling of the crowd. He was young and fabulously wealthy and bearing the grievance of his father's murder. He hadn't been shy about letting it be known that the murder trail led to Damascus. One of his late father's trusted aides had been found to assume the prime ministership on his behalf. Saad would assume that office in his own right after a second parliamentary victory in 2009. But by then, the substance of power was in the hands of Hezbollah and its Syrian and

Iranian backers. In December of that year, Saad Hariri made the
voyage of his political life—the short trip from Beirut to Damascus for a meeting with Bashar al-Assad. He had been forthright
and explicit in accusing the Syrians of killing his father. But he
now had to run Lebanon's affairs and he had to sit down with the
master of the regime in Damascus. The memory of his father had
to be sacrificed at the altar of practicality. Hariri's supporters—the
French, the Americans, the Saudis—could not balance the power
of the Iran-Syria-Hezbollah axis. The Lebanese had not yet
found a way out of Syria's shadow.

THE COSTS OF REBELLIONS are always easy to see: the disruption
of routine, the lost lives and property, the debris of sudden
upheaval. Harder to measure are the costs of a stagnant status
quo, the price paid when societies atrophy and fail to come
up with new solutions to old dilemmas. A decade into his rule,
Bashar's regime had not been toppled and the security apparatus
his father bequeathed him had held firm. In Washington, a new
order had begun when President Barack Obama signaled that the
policy of George W. Bush toward Syria (and Iran) would
be replaced by a policy of "engagement." All the regime in
Damascus—and its counterpart in Iran—would have to do is
unclench its fist.

Damascus was again a diplomatic destination. The Syrian rulers had always pined for American patronage, and this now
appeared within reach. The regime was being rehabilitated—
indeed that process had begun before the onset of the Obama
presidency. In late 2006, the Iraq Study Group—co-chaired by

former Secretary of State James Baker and former Indiana Congressman Lee Hamilton—issued a report to great fanfare. "The situation in Iraq is grave and deteriorating. There is no path that can guarantee success, but the prospects can be improved," the Iraq Study Group dramatically announced. Faith in the American project in Iraq was at a low point, and this blue-ribbon group of high standing sounded the alarm. There was a role for Syria—and Iran—in the rehabilitation of the Iraq position. Syria was to be given incentives, its help sought on stemming "the flow of fundings, insurgents, and terrorists in and out of Iraq." The American consensus on isolating Syria was giving way, the Bush administration had lost the public debate, and the Republican Party's defeat in off-year congressional elections eroded what was left of its authority.

The Syrian regime could only draw the conclusion that it had waited out the "neocons." In April 2007, Speaker of the House Nancy Pelosi made her way to Damascus and called on Bashar al-Assad. But it was a visit by the French President Nicolas Sarkozy in September 2008 that was seen by the rulers in Damascus as an affirmation that they were the "unavoidable nation" in the region, as the Obama administration would label the Syrian regime. The ostracism of Syria occasioned by the assassination of Rafik Hariri in 2005 had effectively ended. The Saudis had no use for Bashar. He had frustrated them in Lebanon, belittled their leaders, and was everything they abhorred—confrontational, lacking in finesse and decorum. He had broken the code of rulers, described his counterparts in the Arab world as "half-men." But the Saudi monarch had opted for a reconciliation. Bashar visited Riyadh in September 2009, and King Abdullah made a landmark visit to Damascus the following month. All was neither forgiven,

nor forgotten, but the desire to separate Syria from Iran had won
out. The Saudi taste for challenging Syria in Lebanon had abated.
The Saudis were no strangers to the doings and the fractures of
Lebanon, but by 2009, they had concluded that the advantages of
Syria in Lebanon could not be surmounted. King Abdullah and
Bashar al-Assad's flight to Beirut aboard the Saudi monarch's
plane in June 2010 was a powerful message to the Lebanese that
Syria retained primacy in their affairs. The tide favored the Syrian
rulers. Changes in two big Western democracies had worked to
their advantage: for George W. Bush there was now Barack
Obama, for Jacques Chirac—Rafik Hariri's friend and diplomatic
patron—there was now Nicolas Sarkozy.

The Assad regime had assets to bring to the game. A diplomatic cable from the U.S. Embassy in Damascus, in early 2009,
puts on display the skills of Syrian intelligence and political operatives. It is February 18 and the new administration in Washington was testing the waters in the region and probing Syria's
readiness for intelligence cooperation. The State Department's
coordinator for counterterrorism, Daniel Benjamin had come to
Damascus with a small group of aides. He is set to meet with
Deputy Foreign Minister Faisal al-Miqdad. But a surprise
awaited him, a "gift" thrown his way, he was told, by President
Assad himself. General Ali Mamlouk, the head of the General
Intelligence Directorate, was there as well. Miqdad said the presence of General Mamlouk should not be taken as a signal that
intelligence and security cooperation had commenced between
the two countries. As in the way of the bazaar, this was just a
teaser, an invitation into the shop. Intelligence cooperation,
Mamlouk observed, would have to wait for progress on "political
issues" between the U.S. and Syria. There was an American need
for Syrian cooperation on the matter of jihadists making their

way to Iraq from Syrian soil; the Syrians would cooperate but were waiting for the Iraqi elections scheduled for March. Benjamin had done academic work on Al Qaeda and Islamist terrorism, and he laid out the American view of the threat to regional order presented by terrorist groups. He said he knew that Syria and the United States differed on Hamas and Hezbollah, and he wanted it understood that the United States still viewed these movements as a threat to the peace of the region.

Mamlouk was proud of the Syrian record in fighting terrorism. Syria had been at this kind of endeavor for thirty years, he said. It had a better record than the United States and other governments because "we are practical and not theoretical." He gave away the essence of his craft, the manner in which he and the other intelligence agencies in his country fought terrorists. "In principle, we don't attack or kill them immediately. Instead we embed ourselves in them and only at the opportune moment do we move." The process of "planting embeds" was subtle and "complex," he added. Yes, it was true some terrorists were slipping into Iraq from Syria, but the two sides can work on this and better results were sure to follow. Syria and the United States had worked together in the past, but Mamlouk took a dim view of that relationship. Were the Americans and the Syrians to embark on a new relationship, the Syrians would have to take the lead. "This is our area, and we know it. We are on the ground, and so we should take the lead." He returned to the subject of Iraq and for transparent reasons: he knew the American need for a stable Iraq. The jihadists who cross into Iraq, he said, come from large Arab and Muslim countries, and Syria was doing its best to round them up and to detain their "local facilitators." He wanted his American interlocutor to know that just last year he had turned over two dozen Saudi jihadists to Prince Muqrin, head of Saudi intelligence. It was a message at

once shrewd but obvious: the Saudis were America's most important Arab ally, but it was Saudi jihadists who were America's
enemies in Iraq.

It was now Miqdad's turn: the man wanted a "political
umbrella" for this cooperation over intelligence matters. Syria
would have to be removed from the list of states sponsoring terrorism, the economic sanctions would have to be lifted, and the
dealings sweetened by allowing Syria to purchase spare parts for
planes and in particular the plane for President Assad. (The plane
was a gift from the emir of Qatar, then a close ally of Bashar.)
This was needed, Miqdad said, to "convince the Syrian people"
that cooperation with the United States was yielding dividends
for Syria. Better days were in the offing, Benjamin told the
Syrians: unlike the preceding administration, the new team in
Washington "did not see counterterrorism as something that was
separate from the rest of U.S. foreign policy or the sole driver of
U.S. foreign policy."

The Damascus regime knew the ways of the world. Its country
was an economic backwater, the foreigners—particularly the
Americans who blew in and out of the region—came for intelligence cooperation, for bargaining over hostages, for signaling that
a new foreign policy for the region was in the making. Old Man
Assad himself had taught that America did not have the patience
or the stomach for long, taxing exertions in the Fertile Crescent.
He had prided himself on ignoring America's "red lines," defying
America's wishes and getting away with it. The Syrians would
take what America had to offer, but the Americans were left in
no doubt that Syria's vital connection to Iran, even to Hezbollah
and Hamas, would not be sacrificed.

The cable traffic from the U.S. Embassy in Damascus in
2009–2010 is filled with optimism that the "reengagement" of

the regime was on track. A new administration was invested in the belief that Syria would mend its ways, and the bureaucracy obliged. As early as April 2009, the reading from Damascus was upbeat. No "grand bargain" had been achieved, one cable of April 6 noted, but there were "positive first steps." No one was thinking of regime change now, and "behavior reform" was the ambition of the day. Congressional delegations were frequent visitors to Damascus. The Syrian staging of these events was skilled, including the coveted audiences with the Syrian ruler and the bits of intelligence about terrorists and infiltrators to Iraq. The Syrian ruler exuded confidence. He spoke as a seasoned observer of Washington's ways. He wished President Obama well, but he despaired of the American system. The four-year cycle of American presidencies frustrated him. It took an American president one year to learn on the job, one year to campaign for a new term, and a mere two years to get anything done.

The self-presentation of Bashar was pitch-perfect. He was a modernist, a secularist bent on fighting political Islam. His wife was a modern woman, and he had come into a political inheritance he was keen to repair. He had an alliance with Iran, but he was open to a deal with the West. His father had been a man of the barracks and a haggler in the old-fashioned way, who spoke through translators and who kept the West at arm's length. Bashar knew French and English; he was no stranger to Western ways. Moderation was always within reach, and dissidents could be released from prison upon the request of American visitors but only if they admitted to their guilt. The regime had all the cards: it could release dissidents of note as it rounded up other critics.

A foreign policy luminary in the Democratic Party, Senate Foreign Relations Committee Chairman John F. Kerry took to the Assad regime and its ruler. It was no secret that Kerry pined to be secretary of state, and he did the next best thing with the onset of the Obama presidency. He became a troubleshooter for the new administration. This brought him to Damascus, which he would visit four times in 2009 and 2010. He was optimistic that a deal could be struck with Bashar al-Assad. The Syrian ruler and his spouse sold the senator on their dream of a prosperous and democratic Syria. Above all, they held out the promise of a moderate Islamic country, and Kerry bought into that promise. It was hard for him to plead the case for Bashar al-Assad, and the eruption in Syria against the regime overwhelmed the Kerry diplomacy. In his defense Kerry would say that he hadn't taken seriously the idea of Bashar as a political "reformer." His was a more limited ambition, he said. He had wanted to explore whether there was a "path" out of Syria's radicalism in foreign policy. Others had gone before him, he said. Former Secretaries of State Henry Kissinger and James Baker had pursued similar policies of engagement with the Damascus regime. He did not regret having tested Syria's intentions; what he regretted was the missed opportunity by Bashar al-Assad. The deplorable policies of the Syrian dictator "may well result in the end of his reign, and he will have no one to blame but himself," Kerry said in June 2011, in the midst of the bloodbath.

The American consular and political officers in Damascus were savvy professionals, and their dispatches about the course of this "reengagement" with the regime were more cautious. One cable on September 10, 2009, took the measure of this new policy, then in its sixth month. "In those six months, we have seen both positive and negative movement by the SARG [Syrian Arab Republic Government]. On core issues—Iran, Hezbollah, Hamas, Iraq, the International Atomic Energy Agency, and Lebanon—the current SARG position has hardened and poses a variety of challenges. At the same time, we have seen some progress in the normalization of our dialogue, between capitals and embassies, and we have the sense that Damascus is keen to continue the dialogue." The Syrians were on home turf, and they could offer the bait of stemming the flow of jihadists into Iraq as they themselves had recruited and trained operatives to sow mayhem in Iraq. Thus it came to light in a February 2010 dispatch that political prisoners had rioted on three occasions because the Syrian government had reneged on a pledge to grant these prisoners freedom upon their return from Iraq. The Syrians were immensely skilled at this kind of thing, as no foreign power could fully master so secretive and alien a setting.

IT WAS ONE THING for the regime of Bashar al-Assad to maneuver its way into the good graces of the United States and France, but the deeper crisis was at home, and that crisis could be discerned in its terrible performance and in the damage incurred by a long-suffering population. Human Rights Watch was on the mark when it described Bashar's first ten years in power as a wasted decade. By every measure that counts: Syria was a backwater, and the damage done to it by Old Man Assad was compounded by the deeds of his son. Unemployment was well over 20 percent, and 32 percent of its people lived below the poverty line. The country ranked 165th (out of 175 nations) in press freedom, 152nd (out of a sample of 152) on the index of democracy, and 19th (out of 22 Arab countries) in economic performance. Syrian universities and academic institutions were a shambles. Bashar had begun the era by releasing political prisoners, but before long he was busy filling the prisons again. A political activist put it well to Human Rights Watch. "In the 1980s, we went to jail without trial. Now, we get a trial, but we still go to jail."

Midway through Bashar's first decade in power, in 2005, a group of civil libertarians, lawyers, and Kurdish dissidents came together to issue a manifesto. The Damascus Declaration was an autopsy of what ailed the country and a program for reform. The inspiration came from blueprints for change that intellectuals and dissidents had put forth in central and eastern Europe in their struggle against dictatorships. There was nothing incendiary in the Damascus Declaration. Its language and demands were mild, but in the context of the tyranny and the monopoly on power by the Baath Party and the intelligence services, it was a bold challenge to that ossified state. The country was in deep crisis, the signatories said, and its people were in need of "self-appraisal." The regime had effectively taken the Syrian people out of public affairs, and its policies in Lebanon had brought about its isolation both at home and abroad. "Opportunism" and "totalitarian thought" had poisoned political life, and a new "social contract" was needed to build a "modern state." A "democratic solution" was needed for the Kurdish question that guarantees that community "cultural and linguistic rights." The emergency laws had to be abolished, those "involuntarily exiled" had to be given the right to an "honorable return" if the country were to turn over a new leaf in its history. The authoritarian state had ended political life, and the leaders who formulated this declaration wanted an open political debate, the release of "popular organizations, federations, trade unions, and chambers of commerce, industry, and agriculture from the custodianship of the state and from party and security hegemony." There was nothing here about overthrowing the regime, no call for Bashar al-Assad to abdicate. But the "despotism"—and the Damascus Declaration used the very word in its final paragraph—could not grant these reforms. The ruler, the intelligence barons, and the old party functionaries were determined to maintain the order they knew.

Syria was under the gaze of outside powers in October 2005, a mere eight months after the assassination of Rafik Hariri in Beirut. For the first time in years, there was pressure on the regime from Paris and Washington. The Saudis had been offended by the Hariri murder, and the old rules of live and let live that worked between Old Man Assad and the House of Saud had ruptured. The security state would read this declaration through the prism of its paranoia and isolation. These dissidents were, by its lights, dividing the ranks of the nation at a time of peril.

CHAPTER FIVE

The Boys of Deraa

S YRIA HAD ITS OFFICIAL PRIDE, and that pride helped blind it to the gathering storm kicked up by the Arab Spring. In late January 2011—a fortnight after the fall of the Tunisian strongman and days after Egyptians had taken to Liberation Square to overthrow their dictatorship—Bashar al-Assad gave an illuminating interview to *The Wall Street Journal.* If the tumult in the region had given him reason for concern, he hid it well. "Syria is stable. Why? Because you have to be strongly linked to the beliefs of the people. This is the core issue. When you have divergence . . . you will have this vacuum that creates disturbance." He was at one with his people, he led a "confrontation" state with Israel, and he was at odds with the United States—all this immunized him against upheaval. Syria would not go the way of Egypt and Tunisia. "If you didn't see the need for reform before what happened in Egypt and Tunisia, it's too late to do any reform. If you want to talk about Tunisia and Egypt, we are outside of this; at the end we are not Tunisians and we are not Egyptians. We are not a copy of each other." He spoke as a young reformer, cast himself as a sorrowful observer of the retrogression that settled upon the region as a whole. "Extremism" has taken root among the Arabs, he observed, and this has resulted in "less creativity, less development, and less openness." And the West has been of no help. The peace process, in motion since

1991, had yielded no dividends. Hope had always issued in failure. He spoke in the familiar language of enlightened autocrats:
he is at the floodgates, saying, "We need flowing water, but how
fast is the flow? If it is very fast, it can be very destructive or you
can have a flood. Therefore, it should be flowing smoothly."

The gatekeeping had not worked. Bashar spoke too soon; six
weeks later, rebellion came Syria's way. There was no Syrian
exceptionalism to this pan-Arab crisis. It did not matter that
Bashar was three decades younger than the Tunisian strongman
and nearly four decades than the Egyptian ruler. In hindsight, it
was inevitable that the caravan of Arab freedom would make its
appearance in Syria. It was there, three decades earlier, that official terror had hatched a monstrous state—and where practically
everything Arabs would come to see in their politics was fore-
shadowed. Modern Syria had always been certain of its place in
the Arab constellation. The Syrians had long insisted that Arab
nationalism had been their gift to other Arabs, that the Egyptians
and other Arabs were newcomers to that idea. The events in
Tunisia, Egypt, and Libya—not to mention the protests in Yemen
and Bahrain—had tantalized and emboldened the Syrians. There
was an old script in Damascus written by Hafez al-Assad: the
struggle against Israel took precedence over all other concerns.
That ruler had had a choice, a man of the Iraqi political class said
to me: he could be an Arab hero against Israel, or an Alawi tyrant.
The choice had been easy to make, and the lesson had been transmitted to his faithful inheritor. Let them eat anti-Zionism, that
inheritance taught. Tell the young that their desire for bread, freedom, and opportunities, and their taste for the world beyond the
walls of the big prison that the regime had erected would have to
wait until the Syrian banners are raised over the Golan Heights.

But the protesters, who conquered their fear and doubt and were willing to go beyond the searing memory of Hama and the cruel 1980s, were reading from a new script. A new country was emerging from hibernation. When the Assads came into their dominion four decades earlier, Syria was a largely rural society with 6 million people. Now the country was urbanized, and its population had swelled to 22 million—which meant some 16 million people had known no other rule than that of the Assads and their security state. This population was perilously young: 50 percent were under 19 years of age, and 57 percent of people under 25 were unemployed.

If history were to repeat itself, the rebellion this time around would have erupted in Hama—the city exacting its revenge for what it had endured three decades earlier and for the neglect it suffered in the intervening years. Homs, Hama's twin city in the central plains, which was larger and had Sunnis, Alawis, and Christians thrown together, might have been another contender.

But history never stands still. The regime, spawned in the countryside and driven by the ambitions and resentments of marginal men, would meet its nemesis nearly half a century later in the very same countryside. The narrator of Khaled Khalifa's exquisite novel, *Dafatir al-Qurbat*, published in 2010, tells of his cousin, a Baath Party functionary, who had quit his forlorn village in the north of Aleppo for a political career in the capital. The cousin had hated the village and couldn't wait to get away from it. He had "spit on its stones when he left, swore to himself that he would never return. His contemporaries remembered that he did not show up for his mother's funeral, he came ten days later, stayed for one evening to receive the faded condolences from the people of his village, and hurried back to his work in the capital" that no one in this village understood or knew anything about. He would come back again, this cousin, because the party had put him up for a seat in parliament from his place of birth. He spoke to the villagers, in one solitary meeting, about the government's "grand victories, about its devotion to the masses, about the old feudalists and capitalists who wanted to destroy the country and turn it into a wasteland to be preyed upon by the crows and to be exploited by the opportunists. He put a special emphasis on the word 'opportunists.' This was a strange word to his listeners, they took it to be some exalted government rank and wanted their children to aspire to it." This was what passed for a political campaign, and the election a rigged formality. The cousin was gone again.

It was Deraa, the administrative center of the agricultural plain of Hawran, by the frontier with Jordan, which had been first to stir. And there had been Dayr az Zawr in the east and Baniyas on the coast. These and other neglected towns had been incubators of the Baath Party and the regime it had spawned. (The people of Dayr az Zawr say that they were visited in 2008 by Bashar al-Assad, the first presidential visit since independence.) The International Crisis Group put it well in an astute analysis of the making of this rebellion. "Ironically, the regime grew out of the very same provinces that today are rebelling against it. In the 1950s and 1960s, the peasantry and provincial petty bourgeoisie saw in the military and Baath Party instruments of social promotion. Hailing from marginal areas such as Hawran, the Mediterranean coast, or Dayr az Zawr, they ultimately turned the tables against a quasi-feudal elite that monopolized political power, land ownership, financial capital, and religious legitimacy. With the 1963 coup d'état, the central seat of power was conquered by the periphery."

But the arteries of the regime had hardened. The arc of the new elite was the all-too-familiar story of how the hitherto excluded carry themselves after coming into new dominions. There were Alawi officers who thrived in the new Syria, and they would not share the spoils they had hoarded, not even with their religious kinsmen. A partnership was forged between the Alawi officers in the army and the security services, and the Sunni merchant class. The children of the senior commanders had done particularly well by that relationship. *Awlad al-sulta* (children of authority), they were called, literally sons of the regime. "Over the years," the International Crisis Group observed, "the regime forgot its social roots, increasingly distancing itself from the peripheral areas from which it came." The gap between city and country widened as the regime grew disinterested in the rural provinces. The presence of the state in the life of the neglected provinces was reduced to the predatory presence and practices of the security services. This was hardly the material for a normal world.

A dozen or so boys from the hinterland town of Deraa, in early March, went out and scribbled some anti-regime graffiti on the walls. There had been a chant making its seductive way through Arab lands. The chant about the people wanting the fall of the regime was rhythmic, and the television broadcasts amplified it. It had been heard in Egypt, Bahrain, Yemen, and Libya. And now this handful of boys, aged 10 to 15, had brought it to the most forbidding of authoritarian settings—the Syrian dictatorship.

On the outskirts of Deraa was a military base that housed the Alawi officers and their families. The presence of the state in the lives of the people of Deraa came in the form of the military and the security services. The boys were picked up, and when the tribal elders and notables of this town went to inquire after them, they were treated with contempt. Forget your children, they were reportedly told. Go home and get new ones, and if you can't we can send your way men who could father new children. When the boys were returned home, it was learned that they had been abused and tortured. Deraa stirred to life, and the city's principal mosque, the Omari Mosque, now served as the gathering place for waves of protesters. The death toll would mount in a hurry, and the regime was both taken by surprise and determined to nip this upheaval in the bud. The security forces began with water cannons and were soon operating with orders to kill, firing on protesters and funeral processions alike. Snipers made their appearance in Deraa, and many of the victims suffered head, neck, and chest wounds. Deraa came under siege. It was to be punished for breaching the silence of the land. It didn't matter to the forces of order that countless protesters were carrying olive branches, unbuttoning their shirts to show that they had no weapons, and chanting "peaceful, peaceful." Deraa would suffer acute shortages of food, water, and medicine. Its communication with the outside world was shut down. When other towns sent people to help in Deraa, they, too, came under attack. The security forces opened fire on medical personnel attempting to care for the wounded. Four weeks into this siege, the call to prayer was banned. The mosques were commandeered by the security forces and desecrated. There were empty alcohol bottles, and on the walls of several mosques there was graffiti mocking the faith, "Your God is Bashar." "There is no God but Bashar" was the most defiling and offensive to the believers. No Muslim soldier would go that far, the people of Deraa concluded. These were Alawi schismatics who had done this, and the mosques were not theirs to honor. The first ten days were the bloodiest; at least 200 of Deraa's people had fallen.

Deraa had shown the way. It had shamed and emboldened other towns. Baniyas, Latakia, Idlib, and Tartus took up the banner of rebellion. The "peaceful, peaceful" chant had been to no avail. By late May, according to Human Rights Watch, 887 people had been killed, 418 of them in Deraa alone. The provincial backwater had been made to pay for its defiance. The course of the rebellion was to show the extent to which this regime had been caught flat-footed by the changes that had washed upon the population. "Some of the security people leading this effort," a regime insider told the researchers of the International Crisis Group, "are 30 years behind the time. They believe that some of the methods in the early 1980s still apply." The protesters were not struggling alone in anonymity, as technology had altered the terms of this fight. "Every Syrian with a mobile phone can turn himself into a live satellite television broadcaster," the regime insider said. "How can we resort to such means when we are facing 24 million satellite televisions in our midst?" The security forces had been trained on old methods of repression. They could not be "reformed" or changed in the midst of this new battle. The regime was obtuse. It sent into the streets *minhebek* ("we love you") demonstrations hailing the ruler, but no one was taken in or cowed by these displays of manufactured consent.

In the time-honored practice of regimes that history catches unprepared, the ruling order alternated brutality with promises of reform. In a dizzying and frantic rolling out of official initiatives, the ruler appointed a new prime minister when the country knew that the prime minister possessed no genuine power. To placate the Kurds, a pledge was made to make Nowruz a national holiday.

The Sunni majority had to be given a concession, so this most secular of regimes announced the launching of a new Islamic television channel. The city of Baniyas had been roused by the firing of 1,200 teachers and school employees who donned the hijab; they were reinstated. The regime was headed into treacherous economic waters, but salaries were raised, subsidies were augmented, and the wheat procurement prices were raised to gain the support of the farmers. Plans had been readied to slash the expensive fuel subsidies, but they were now shelved. There was an emergency law in place since 1963—this was a way of life, not some temporary decree—and it would now be lifted. The real terror was off the books, administered by the security forces, tanks, and helicopters against the population. The lifting of the emergency decrees was of no value for ordinary men and women running for their lives into neighboring countries. When these troubles erupted, it was reasonable for the custodians of the regime to assume that they had in their arsenal a measure of popular goodwill toward the man at the helm. The ruler had not been particularly egregious as he had stayed above the fray. Doctor Bashar, it was thought, would ward off the troubles.

Bashar would deliver three speeches as the storm gathered force—on March 30, April 16, and June 20. The first was delivered before a sycophantic parliament, and Bashar showed the extent of his isolation from reality. There was smugness in his delivery and a vanity about his regime that the unfolding fight in the country would make more absurd still. He looked beyond Syria. The "Arab condition," he said, vindicated Syria and its policies. Syria had shown the way, and it had refused to be "domesticated." Syria was unlike the other countries. It had "certain characteristics" in its conduct at home that set it apart from nearby countries, and it would maintain its course. "Today, there is a new fashion which they call revolutions. We do not call them so because we think this is mostly a popular condition." There were "unmet needs" in Syria, but the regime was well on its way toward dealing with them. "Sedition" had overtaken the quest for reform, because Syria was in the crosshairs as a target for conspiracies. "Incitement" had come from outside. "Fake information, voices, images, etc., they forged everything." The unnamed conspirators had been skilled, they used the "sectarian element," they sent "masked people to neighborhoods with different sects living in them, knocking on people's doors and telling each that the other sect has already attacked and are on the streets, in order to get a reaction. And it worked for a while. But we were able to nip the sedition in the bud. . . . Then they used weapons. They started killing people at random, because they knew when there is blood it becomes more difficult to solve the problem." He hadn't yet discovered the whole structure of the conspiracy, but it was "highly organized" and linked to "some countries abroad." The security forces had been given orders "not to harm any Syrian citizens." But things had "moved to the street" and Syrian blood was shed. It was Syria's fate to be visited at this time by sedition and crisis. The Arab world had been in "a state of collapse and submission to America." Syria had resisted the American project, and the price was this upheaval. Reform had been in the works and had issued from within; it was not a reflection of this "new wave sweeping the region." Bashar's regime had tried to learn from the experience of other countries. Tunisia had been instructive, he said. His regime had looked into the Tunisian experience and learned that the "uneven geographical distribution of wealth" was a big source of trouble, but Syria had done its best to avoid that defect. This crisis might be "a blessing in disguise." Syria was being tested, and it was sure to prevail. This sedition will not bring this proud country to its knees. "The Holy Quran says, 'sedition is worse than killing,' and all are called upon to bury this sedition in defense of the homeland."

Bashar al-Assad hadn't been known for Islamic piety, and this exhortation from the Quran has long been favored by sultans and rulers faced with rebellions. The speech fell with a thud, and the men of the regime knew it. A fortnight later, the ruler gave it another try. The theme of this new speech, in mid-April, was "dignity." Syria, he pronounced, owed its people dignity in the conduct of its officials and in the performance of its economy. The blood that had been shed over the preceding four weeks was Syrian blood. He had been grieved by the loss, and all those who fell—civilians, security forces, and soldiers alike—were "martyrs." A new cabinet was in place and would take some time to master its brief, but it had been given its mission: the lifting of the emergency decrees, in place since 1963, and the drafting of laws that would permit and codify the right to civil protest and demonstrations—these were evidence of a desire for reform. There was a catch-22 at work: once these laws are codified, there would be no need for demonstrations because the Syrian people, by their temperament, were a "civilized, disciplined people who abhorred chaos and hooliganism." The "space for freedom" would be expanded in the days to come, and Syria would provide a rebuttal, a "historical answer to those Orientalists who had written so much about the Arabs in the past and said that this region, by its makeup, is incapable of democratic development." The needs of the Syrian people were limitless, he added. "The average citizen wants justice, roads, water, development, health care, education." There were so many young people in need of jobs, there was the country's very high birthrate, and all these were monumental challenges. There had been four years of drought, and the agricultural sector and the countryside had suffered as a result.

If the theme of the first speech had been about the "conspiracies" hatched for the country, this one was a laundry list about what ailed it at home—corruption, "electronic government," decentralization, the modesty required of public officials in dealing with the citizenry. The "reformer" and the modernizer, the head of the country's computer society, the chief technocrat, Dr. Bashar, was back. In the streets, it was messier. He was coming into ownership of the repression, but this was a bow to the new reality and a recognition that his speech a fortnight earlier had not worked.

The third speech, on June 20—jinxed by the precedent of Hosni Mubarak giving three speeches before the curtain came down on him—was given at Damascus University. Gone was the antiseptic tone of the second speech. There was a bloody insurgency, and he had to speak to it. He returned to the theme of the conspiracies being hatched for the country. "Conspiracies are like germs, which increase every moment." There were three types of people out in the streets, he said, those with legitimate needs, the lawbreakers, and those with an extremist ideology, which the country had faced for decades. He reached for precision. He was surprised, he said, to learn that those wanted by the law, "people of sedition," numbered 64,000. The number represented a big challenge to the government, but the government will not exact any revenge. A fair-minded distinction would be made between protesters and saboteurs. The protesters, in the middle of this grim time, had found a capacity for satire and humor. They feasted on the talk of germs. The Syrian people, one banner proclaimed, are in need of a new doctor. There had been that other embattled despot, Qaddafi in Libya, who had dubbed his people rats, and a connection was made with that struggle. "The Syrian germs salute the Libyan rats," another banner had it.

The speeches were overwhelmed by the reality. Bashar had earned for himself by now the title of *saffah* (blood shedder). If there had been hope that the ruler would step away from the carnage, rise above it, and rescue his regime, it now belonged to the past. The distinction between the Assad father and son was being erased.

We get an unadorned and spare portrait of the onset of the rebellion from the diary of a young participant in the protests in the coastal city of Baniyas. That city was the second theater of trouble after Deraa. It had risen in protest against the ministry of education firing a large number of schoolteachers and employees who donned the hijab. This was a mixed city in Alawi country, with the Alawis constituting 65 percent of the population. Sunni sensibility had been offended by the ban on the hijab. But there was more: there was a big oil refinery here, and the Alawis virtually monopolized all the available jobs and recruited fellow Alawis from as far away as Homs. Baniyas had an articulate young Sunni cleric, Shaykh Anas al-Ayrout, and he gave his passion and leadership to the eruption against the regime. Ayrout was the "head of the sedition," the authorities said.

The diary of this young protester commences the night of April 2, not long after the start of the rebellion. It is past midnight and the electricity and all means of communication are cut off. Fear grips the city in anticipation of an attack by the security forces. This protester leaves his home and walks through the streets, where others were doing the same. Thoughts of Hama in 1982 were on the minds of many during this troubled night. After dawn prayers, a former military recruit active in the protests embarks on a quick inspection of the city streets and returns to tell those manning makeshift barricades and checkpoints that there was no trace of the *shabiha* (the security forces). Some of the barricades were taken down, but the residents had stayed outdoors. At five in the morning, the attack came. Seven cars packed with armed men tore through the city at great speed, firing at random at homes and mosques. A number of people were wounded, and one was to die a week later in the hospital, becoming "the first martyr of Baniyas." The city residents answered in kind, or tried to. They fired at the assailants with hunting rifles and old weapons. Our narrator does not know if any of the attackers had been hit. Two of the cars were damaged, and they were pulled into the central city square and set on fire. On one of the cars, the protesters wrote, "Remember, you are in Baniyas, not in Israel."

By mid-afternoon, the shabiha and the security forces had begun to converge on an Alawite neighborhood at the outskirts of the city. A hundred men or so from a unit of the regular army suddenly turned up. On their colonel's orders, the troops began alternating their fire between the Alawite quarter and a Sunni neighborhood nearby. Under the cover provided by the army unit, snipers from the shabiha and the security forces made their way to the rooftops in the Alawite quarter. This went on until the early evening. Our narrator was told on good authority that the colonel had fired point-blank at six of his soldiers for disobeying his orders; three of them died instantly. One army officer had been killed in the fight, and another had lost his legs when a young fighter from Baniyas threw a stick of dynamite into his armored car. In an illuminating detail, the narrator tells us that the officer who lost his legs was seen on television not long after the attack. With his Alawi accent that can't be lost on all Syrians, the officer had acknowledged the strong nerves of the fighter who had charged the armored car, opened its door, and placed a stick of dynamite inside, before he ran away.

In the evening, the two Alawi neighborhoods in Baniyas, Al-Qusur and Al-Qawz, were completely deserted. Their people had fled to a mountain nearby. Some men of Baniyas with standing and ties to the regime attempted to negotiate a peace agreement on behalf of the city. They agreed that the shabiha and the security forces would leave the city and that the regular army would take their place. The security forces pulled out, taking the furniture of their headquarters with them. In the morning, a small military unit arrived and picked up the bodies of the three soldiers who had been killed by the colonel. Three wounded soldiers were taken by the young men of Baniyas to the local hospital for treatment.

On the morning of April 3, the army surrounds Baniyas. When some tanks attempted to enter the city, the people came out in protest, and the tanks pulled back. The shabiha and the security forces besieged the city, cutting off provisions, arresting anyone caught in their net, and paralyzing normal life and commerce. The public buildings and the municipality offices were shuttered; most of the employees were Alawis who had quit the city. Schools were closed, and fear gripped many Sunni families as well, tempting them to make their way through the checkpoints manned by the security forces.

Baniyas foretold the course of this rebellion: the neighborhoods divided along confessional lines, the Alawis who ran the city deserted it for the safety of the mountain, the forces of order fomented trouble between the sects. The Syrian affair would be much deadlier than the other Arab rebellions.

CHAPTER SIX

The Phantoms of Hama

THE PROTESTERS ARRAYED against the regime of Bashar al-Assad had a premonition of what was to come. They gave their Friday protests on July 29 a name: Your Silence Is Killing Us. It was said that they had in mind the cities of Aleppo and Damascus, which had hitherto stood largely aloof from the rebellion while the cities of Homs and Hama paid dearly for their defiance. But the protesters made no secret that they had the League of Arab States in mind as well. At home and in Cairo, the domicile of the Arab League, they had carried coffins with the name of the League scribbled on them. And they would have been in their right to include powers beyond the Arab world, for the regime in Damascus had killed with abandon and without incurring a heavy price in the process.

On Sunday, the regime struck. This was the day before the holy month of Ramadan, and the rulers and the protesters alike were preparing for a month of agitation. Scores were killed across the country. The Syrian League for Human Rights estimates that at least 120 people were killed, the single bloodiest day since the uprising began five months earlier. In an ominous foreshadowing of what was to come, in the early hours of dawn, the army and the security forces entered the city of Hama. The dispatches from the city reported there were bodies scattered in the streets. For several weeks, it had been thought that the city was off-limits, because of the burden of the bloody history between Hama and the regime. It was here in 1982 that the military ruler, Hafez al-Assad, marked his regime with its defining cruelty—and sectarianism. The Muslim Brotherhood had made a stand here, and it was doomed. The man at the helm was in the fight to the finish. The Brotherhood had dragged this city of artisans and shopkeepers into a struggle it could not win. The insurgents had made their stand in the warrens of the Old City, but no mercy was shown them. Between 20,000 and 30,000 people perished, and thousands disappeared. Practically every family in Hama had a vendetta of its own against the dictatorship.

Cities beget legends, and Hama had always regarded the world beyond its confines with a jaundiced eye. A foreign traveler, Robin Fedden, in *Syria: An Historical Appreciation* (1946), described Hama as a city of "faith and feudalism." "The West was less present here than in any of the other large towns in Syria. Islam colors and conditions its temper, and there can be few places outside the Holy Cities of Arabia where the faith has remained so aggressive and fanatic. Even the position of the town symbolizes its enclosure in Islam and the past. The Orontes eats its way—no other phrase describes it—through the dry plain, and the windings of the river are overshadowed by cliffs and hish escarpments. Hama, lying on the river, is thus in a sunken world." The feudalism—four families had owned much of the agricultural land and dominated the religious life—would be torn asunder in the years to come. Hama's own rebels would take part in that destruction of all patterns of power and domination. The rule of the four families would be broken by the early 1960s. There remained the faith, wary and sharpened for combat, on the lookout for outsiders bearing radical, new disruptions of settled ways.

The 1982 massacre wasn't Hama's first brush with trouble. A good generation earlier, in 1964, a year after the Baath Party came to power, Hama had risen in defiance of the Baathist-military regime, wanting nothing to do with the socialism of the Baath and its irreverence toward Islam and its place in public life. The privileged position of the minorities—Alawis, Druze, Ismailis—in that regime put it on a collision course with the Muslim Brotherhood and its sympathizers among the Hamawis. The city was brought to heel after a lengthy general strike. The militants of the Brotherhood sought shelter in Hama's largest mosque; the mosque was shelled and the rebellion was crushed. But the roots of the Muslim Brotherhood ran deep in Hama, and there were intermittent troubles in the 1970s.

When these protests erupted in March 2011, Hama had taken its time and sat out the first wave of troubles—it was a haunted city for the rulers and Hama's people alike. For Bashar, Hama summoned the ghost of his father and the stigma of being at one with him. No doubt Bashar owed it all to his father. The reign that came his way was his father's gift to him. He had been bequeathed what was for all practical purposes a kingdom of his own. His father had done it the hard way—guile and terror side by side. But Bashar aspired to something new: the mantle of reform, the promise of changing this drab dictatorship. But trouble came to Hama, as it was bound to. On Friday, April 22, a good long month into these troubles, Hama had its first major protest. This was a fortress of the Sunni street, the country's fourth-largest city. On June 3, the security forces clashed with protesters who had taken to the streets of Hama, and nearly 70 people were killed. The regime had tested Hama's resolve and then suddenly pulled back, as though spooked by bloodshed in that city, by its very symbolism. The government pulled off a veritable disappearing act. Hama was left to administer its own affairs, neighborhood councils rushed to fill the void, the city savored the taste of independence, and checkpoints and barriers were erected in preparation for another showdown with the government. On July 8, Hama held the largest protests to date in this upheaval and gave a rousing reception to U.S. Ambassador Robert Ford, who braved his way there. Flowers and olive branches greeted the American envoy, who had come with the French ambassador, to signal something of an American break with the Assad regime.

The uneasy peace between the rebellious city and the rulers was not destined to last. The preceding month had witnessed bloody battles in Homs, the other big city in the central plains. Now the "immunity" granted Hama was set aside, as the regime was bent on retrieving the ground it had lost. Hama was too big to cede to the rebellion. The assault gave away the regime's mounting frustration and its eagerness to preempt the disobedience that the month of Ramadan promised to bring with it. The religious impasse between the Alawi regime and the (largely) Sunni opposition stalked this rebellion. The rituals of Ramadan, the evening prayers after breaking the fast, the gatherings in mosques at night after the heat of the summer days, could only mean greater troubles. Fiercely secular if only because the Alawis are schismatics and heterodox, and beyond the pale for mainstream Sunnis, the regime now sought Islamic cover. A new satellite television channel, Noor al-Sham, was launched with strictly religious material, propagating the regime's message of politico-religious obedience and avoidance of political matters.

The quiescent religious establishment that answered to the regime was called upon to preach the virtues of obedience. Muhammad Abdul Sattar al-Sayyid, the minister of religious endowments and a regime functionary, announced that the month of Ramadan was sure to mark the "beginning of the end" for the protests, and that the "crisis had already passed never to return." More importantly, the country's senior cleric, Muhammad Said al-Buti, based in the Umayyad Mosque in Damascus—Syria's most storied and prestigious mosque—was given what must have been a bitter assignment to swallow: to go out and give religious sanction to the regime's repression. The protests, this obliging cleric opined, were not inspired by a desire for reform. They are "the work of people who aim to cripple Syria. Those who want to bring down the regime want to bring down Islam." He had seen "documents and reports" that prove beyond doubt that "our enemies do not wish us well, they don't want our Islamic civilization to flourish, they seek to destroy our Islamic culture."

Now traditional Sunni Islam counsels obedience to the rulers, the avoidance of *fitna* (sedition). It preaches a limited, hemmed-in role for the *ulama* (the religious class), restricting it to "commanding right and forbidding evil." But this measure of supplication before a presumably godless regime that had warred against religion and shown it little if any deference must have been difficult to offer. Shaykh Buti and his peers in the religious establishment were in no position to cap the volcano. The protesters knew these ulama for what they are, *ulama al-nizam* (the clerics of the regime). Buti may have been old and learned, but the rebels had identified him as a tool of the regime, and there were Sunni preachers like him elsewhere in Syria's cities who had been written off by those who had come to topple the Assad government.

Hama put up the resistance it could. Its young people answered the regime's armor and tanks with sticks and iron bars, the burning of tires, and *takbeer* chants ("Allahu Akbar," God is Great). In a country with a deep religious schism between the forces of

the regime, and a popular opposition that had broken with its
rulers, this invocation had a power and a poignancy all its own.

THE REBELLION had a distinct geography, and a distinct confessional geography at that. This was a socioeconomic revolt,
with a difference. The finest and most authoritative account of
this dimension of the rebellion had been provided by Fabrice
Balanche, a French political geographer with an intimate and rare
knowledge of Syria. Balanche had spent a decade in Syria and
Lebanon, and his book *Le Region Alaouite et Le Pouvoir Syrien*
(2006) was an eclectic work of geography and sociology, a study
of "socio-space," he called it. In his hands, the mixture of territory
and community at the heart of Greater Syria was laid out with
care and precision. An essay in 2011, "The Geography of the
Syrian Revolt," was informed by that deep immersion and knowledge of Syrian political and religious materials, of that deadly
intersection of geography and sectarian identity.

Balanche began his essay where this revolt began—in Deraa,
"150 kilometers south of Damascus," the geographer specifies. It
made its way to the coastal cities of Baniyas and Latakia, the
outskirts of Damascus, and then Homs, Hama, and the smaller
towns of Rastan, Talbisseh, Maaret al-Noman, Jisr al-Shughour,
and Idlib, before reaching the province of Dayr az Zawr in July.
These were "neglected" places, bypassed in the transition from
the command economy of Old Man Assad to the new "open"
economy of his son. But this rebellion, "in its immense majority,"
had erupted in the territories of the Sunni Arabs, Balanche writes.
The Kurds, Sunnis themselves, had stayed largely aloof from the
upheaval, had risen in 2004, had been cruelly repressed, and had

fought alone against Damascus. The other minorities—Druze, Ismailis, Christians, Alawis—had remained on the sidelines or, of course, supported the regime. This was not Tunisia or Egypt. "Territorial identity" mattered here, putting into question the unity of this odd nation-state. The protests that had begun in Deraa stopped at the borders of Soueida, the neighboring capital of the Druze.

The Hawran province, the countryside encompassing Deraa, had not been innately rebellious, Balanche maintains. In the 1960s, it had been a beneficiary of the Baath conquest of power. "Agrarian reform"—the breakup of large estates owned by absentee landlords—had worked in Hawran's favor. Its population swelled from 180,000 inhabitants in 1960 to 900,000 in 2010. Hawran gave its loyalty to the regime and its ambitious youth found their way into the cadres of the Baath, but demography shattered the peace. A third generation now wanted state patronage, but the state had withdrawn. It had little if anything to offer. Water was scarce, its distribution subject to the whims of the bureaucracy and riddled with corruption. It was even worse in the north, a setting akin to John Steinbeck's *The Grapes of Wrath*, Balanche writes. The villages did not rebel, the villagers had long quit these places for larger provincial towns, and these were places that would figure prominently in the protests. The unrest varied from one neighborhood to another. In Latakia—a coastal city crucial to the Alawi custodians of power—the prosperous neighborhoods (*les beaux quartiers*) sat out the protests. It was the impoverished neighborhood of Ramal Falstini that gave the regime trouble, and it was shelled by gunboats from the sea. It was the same in Rif Dimashq, the countryside around Damascus; Douma, a large suburb that had seen rapid population growth, had to be subdued by force. In the fabled Ghouta, once a paradise

of gardens on the periphery of Damascus, the poorer neighborhoods in the southwest were filled with squatters and people of
modest means who grew restive. In the northwest, the middle
classes and the bureaucrats were at peace with the order of power.

Physical proximity to the Alawi homeland, Balanche observes,
was a factor in the intensity of the protests. The Alawi territory
lay between the Mediterranean and the Orontes, with Jebel
Ansariyah and the coast at its base. French benevolence, and then
the power of the regime, had enabled the Alawis to come into
city life. The coastal cities of Latakia, Baniyas, Jableh, and Tartus
had acquired Alawi majorities. Tell Khalakh, a troubled town on
the western edge of the Homs governorate, had a Sunni majority,
but the villages around it were Alawi lands. In the big city of
Homs, the Alawi newcomers had become a quarter of the population thanks to state patronage. And the Alawis congregated in
their own neighborhoods, the communal fault lines that separated
them from the Sunni strongholds becoming lines of trouble and
strife. Proximity bred animus and antagonism.

Balanche's analysis distinguishes between mixed cities—
Homs, Baniyas, etc.—and encircled ones—like Damascus and
Aleppo. His cartography makes abundantly clear why Damascus
and Aleppo stayed outside the rebellion. The regime could not
alter the demography of these two huge cities—it did not have
the Alawi population for so ambitious an undertaking. It did the
next best thing; it placed military camps and loyal Alawi migrants
at the strategic approaches to both cities. In Aleppo, the regime
was helped by the Arab-Kurdish fault line that ran through this
northern metropolis, and by the traditional antagonism that pitted the urban Aleppine population against the surrounding countryside. At the end of June, the protesters had called upon the

rural population to descend on Aleppo for a general strike, and this had backfired. Aleppo had opted for quiescence.

Hafez al-Assad, the man who put this regime together, rightly understood that his survival and that of this minoritarian dominion rested on the cohesiveness of his own Alawi community, and on keeping the Sunnis divided among themselves and willing to live and let live with the regime. The son had not been brilliant. He had antagonized—and awakened—enough Sunni resentments to put this dominion at risk. To be sure, not all Sunnis had rebelled against him; a tidal wave would have overwhelmed his dictatorship. There were divisions of class and geography that still ran through the Sunni population, there was the age-old separation between city and country, and the middle classes of Aleppo and Damascus bristled at the idea that they would be led by provincials.

The toll of the rebellion in lives lost throws a floodlight on the neglect of the provinces and the alienation between the rulers and the peripheral places from where they had risen. Human rights monitors and nongovernmental organizations within the country estimated that 3,000 people had been killed by the end of the rebellion's sixth month. (The United Nations' estimates were 2,600.) The grief had not been randomly felt, and some population centers had been disproportionally hurt. Homs, the third-largest city, with its tangled demography, a Sunni majority with a substantial Alawi minority, fared the worst: 761 people had fallen. Deraa had by far the largest fatalities measured by population density: 594 victims. In Idlib and the countryside to its northwest, the toll was 319. Hama, in the public mind the nerve center of the rebellion, lost 350 people. The numbers confirm the widespread belief that Damascus and Aleppo had remained on the margins of the upheaval: ninety had been killed in Damascus, forty-four in Aleppo. These two cities had made their grudging peace with the regime. There was no love lost for it, but an unease with the rebellion and a wary sense that the country might be in for a cruel choice: this regime, with all its defects, or the uncertainties of a drawn-out civil war.

Damascus had its own inhibitions. Here, the regime took no chances. It would ride out the rebellion and survive in Damascus, or it would perish. The full might of this despotism was deployed in the capital. The city had done relatively well by the regime, the presence of the forces of order was heavy, and it stood to reason that Damascus would hesitate in the face of the rebellion. To be sure, all was not well in Damascus, and its people were not immune to the stirrings in the country. On August 27, the Night of Destiny, in the holy month of Ramadan, where prayers and entreaties have a great force to them, the city's most revered cleric, Shaykh Oussama al-Rifaai—he hailed from clerical nobility and was the imam of a mosque named for his family—came under physical attack in his mosque by the security forces. It was known that he and his younger brother, Sariya, a cleric as well, were no fans of the regime. That day in August, one of Shaykh Oussama's followers was killed in the melee, many were wounded, and others were taken into custody. Shaykh Oussama himself was wounded, and his devotees were treated to a YouTube posting of him with his head bandaged and his white *thoub* caked with blood. The Rifaais were immensely popular in the souks of Damascus. The more prominent of the merchants were backers of the Rifaai charities and network of mosques. There was talk then of a Damascus *zilzal* (earthquake), and there was unmistakable anger that so revered a man had been subjected to so offensive a treatment. But the earthquake did not materialize and the Rifaais pulled back, as

did the regime. The Rifaais knew well the temper of the Damascus bazaar. There was no taste for a risky confrontation. The
merchants grumbled and let it be known that there had been a
transgression of the proper norms of conduct.

Aleppo and Damascus came under intense scrutiny and criti-
cism. To the protesters in cities and towns at the receiving end of
this merciless crackdown, these two cities had bartered their soul
in return for safety and ease. "The people of Damascus are not
like they used to be in the past," Muhammad Yaaqubi (born in
1962), who had taught theology at the Umayyad Mosque, said
from exile. "How much longer can we tolerate the shedding of
the blood of our brothers and the violation of daughters? Have
the chocolate and the fast food produced a new kind of man?"
The burden of Damascus was heavy, this scholar exhorted, for if
its people took to the streets "this regime and this ruling family
would fall in a matter of days."

From exile in Saudi Arabia, Muhammad Ali Sabuni, an older
scholar and a man of Aleppo, voiced his disappointment in the
city of his birth. Aleppo had not come to the aid of other cities,
he noted. Its people were risking "divine retribution," punishment
in the hereafter, and support of this rebellion was a "religious
obligation." Sabuni, now 81 years of age, had once been a scholar
of high standing in Aleppo and close to the Muslim Brotherhood.
Five decades of exile in Saudi Arabia had not lessened his interest
in Aleppo's ways.

Yaaqubi's laments about "chocolate and fast food" come close
to the heart of the matter. As the researcher Thomas Pierret
notes, a decade of economic liberalization had been kind to the
Sunni business class. The stability the regime offered was a better
bet than a rebellion that carried with it the risk of social upheaval.
There was no unity among the Sunnis, Pierret reminds us. Class

differences and the differences between the cities and the countryside ran through the Sunni majority. In the ranks of that
devout bourgeoisie, the unease with the Alawi rulers yielded to
economic interests.

By the end of August, well into the rebellion's sixth month, a
case of "Libya envy" could be read in the pamphleteering and
second thoughts of the opposition. NATO had helped deliver the
Libyans out of their tyrant's grip. Fortunate for the break that
came their way, the Libyans hadn't stood on ceremony. They
took the help and were quite vocal in expressing their gratitude.
They paid no heed to those among the Arabs who warned them
of the schemes of the Western powers on their homeland. They
were willing to risk it. The Syrians were hampered by their pride,
not that NATO forces were on their way to Damascus, awaiting
a green light from the Syrian opposition. The modern political
history of Syria was the history of Arab nationalism: its stirring
call in the final years of the Ottoman Empire, the usages it served
as it knit together a nation-state of diverse and often feuding
communities, the weapon it was against the French mandatory
power in the interwar years, and the ideology that both propelled
and frustrated Syrian political life after independence. This
exalted idea of Syria's Arab mission stood in the way of the forthright appeal for foreign help. In what had become standard
practice for the rebellion, a special name was given to Friday,
September 9: the Friday for International Protection. The Syrians
pined for foreign (Western) help, but were at the same time keen
to insist on the sovereignty of their country. They wanted no
foreign troops or foreign boots on the ground. The more prag-
matic among them said they would settle for a no-fly zone. But
that provision would not have altered the terms of the contest in
their midst. Decades of anti-Western indoctrination and a culture

shared by the rulers and oppositionists alike had done their damage. The protesters pleading for "international" protection were made timid by their own estrangement from those in a position to provide the protection.

Wise to the ways of the world, the Syrians hadn't expected an Arab cavalry to come to the rescue, and they were resigned to the relative silence of the Arab world in the face of their ordeal. A placard carried by a demonstrator had ample wisdom: "To the Arab League, Are we not Arab?" The protesters drew a measure of solace from the condemnation of the regime by the Saudi King Abdullah earlier in August. Throwing caution and official reserve to the wind, the Saudi ruler had described the regime in Damascus as a "killing machine." But the opponents of the regime despaired of their fellow Arabs. They had seen the secretary-general of the Arab League, an Egyptian diplomat, meet with their ruler and leave with some mild talk about the case for political reform. The Arab League had no military divisions to deploy, so the Syrians could ignore its entreaties. Syria was successfully trading on its status as a "frontline" state against Israel—even as it kept the most orderly border with Israel since the disengagement accords worked out by U.S. Secretary of State Henry Kissinger in 1974. This was not the isolated and erratic Qaddafi regime. It mastered the tricks of the Arab political order and exuded disdain for Arabs daring to judge its behavior. When an emergency meeting of the Arab foreign ministers on August 28 called on Damascus to "stop the shedding of blood and submit to the rule of reason before it is too late," the Syrian rulers dismissed the appeal. They said they will totally disregard it "as though it had never been made."

The Damascus regime was lucky for the country's borders— Lebanon, Jordan, Israel, Iraq, and Turkey. No rescue mission was in the offing. No foreign power wanted a military operation in that tinderbox. A firecracker would set the neighborhood ablaze, a shrewd diplomat from the Gulf observed of Syria's place in so volatile a setting. Israel was ambivalent throughout, and rightly stayed on the sidelines. There was no love lost for a regime that gave Iran access to the Mediterranean and was allied with Hezbollah and Hamas. But the Damascus regime was a known entity, and better the devil you know than the one you don't. The Syrian rulers were not subtle: as they faced this deadly challenge to their regime, they were to make a naked appeal to Israel. They had not allowed foreign reporters access to their country, but they were to make an exception. An invitation was issued to *The New York Times* reporter Anthony Shadid, who was covering the Syrian troubles from Beirut. A meeting in Damascus was granted Shadid with Rami Makhlouf, Bashar's maternal cousin and a businessman who embodied crony capitalism and sat astride much of Syria's economy. There was a message to Israel, and Makhlouf was the perfect messenger. He was from the inner circle of the House of Assad, but possessing a measure of deniability because he was not an official of the state. "If there is no stability here, there's no way there will be stability in Israel. No way and nobody can guarantee what will happen after, God forbid, anything happens to this regime." Asked if a threat of war was being made, Makhlouf equivocated. "I didn't say war. What I'm saying is don't let us suffer, don't put a lot of pressure on the president, don't push Syria to do anything it is not happy to do." (Nine months after this interview, in February 2012, Shadid died of an asthma attack in Syria. He had made an unauthorized trip, and an allergy to horses cost this gifted reporter his life.)

The ruling cabal had its own view of American policy: it was shaped, if not dictated, by Israel. Syria is of course no match for

Israel, but it could disturb Israel's peace and plunge U.S.-Middle East diplomacy into a deep crisis. "We will not go out, leave on our boat. We will sit here. We will fight until the end," Makhlouf grandly proclaimed.

The reading of Syrian tea leaves is a thriving Israeli industry. For reasons of intellectual curiosity and self-defense, Syria has engaged Israeli academics, defense experts, and policy-makers alike. A deal with Damascus was always on the horizon, often a potential substitute for the more difficult accommodation with the Palestinians. Rami Makhlouf had his brief, and his view, as it happened, had a good measure of support in Israel. For one, there had been a deep-seated intellectual skepticism in Israeli intellectual and political circles about the unsettling political changes brought about by the Arab Spring. The peace accords that Israel had made with its Arab neighbors had been made by strongmen: Anwar al-Sadat and Hosni Mubarak in Egypt, Yasser Arafat in the Palestinian territories, and the Hashemite monarchy in Jordan. True, no binding peace accord had been made with the Syrians, but the Assads had delivered the most quiet of borders. There was no way of knowing who and what would replace this Syrian regime. Populism and chaos could threaten that subtle working relationship developed over four decades. Makhlouf, and the ruler who gave him his mission, wanted this message assimilated in Israel and transmitted to Washington. It was a well-choreographed play: a regime in Damascus that gave sanctuary to the most die-hard of Hamas's leaders, and that was a strong ally of Hezbollah in Lebanon, still had room to maneuver vis-à-vis Israel. There were Israelis, Minister of Defense Ehud Barak reportedly among them, who thought that their world would be better off if a Syrian regime that provided Iran access to the Mediterranean were to be toppled. But on balance, the fear of the unknown appeared to offer a more reliable course.

Turkey's behavior was something of a puzzle. A dozen or so years earlier, the Syrians and the Turks were on the edge of war. Syria had given sanctuary and material support to Turkey's dreaded enemy, the Kurdistan Workers Party (or PKK) and its leader Abdullah Ocalan. In 1998, Ankara dispatched a significant force to the border with Syria. The Syrians had backed down and expelled Ocalan. A new Islamist regime had come to power in Turkey in 2002, and it had drawn closer to Syria. Trade and tourism across the border had flourished. Turkey had stepped forth as a mediator between Syria and Israel. Bashar himself had said there were three important powers in the region—Iran, Turkey, and Syria, in that order—and he had given his own leadership high marks for being in such exalted company. Ankara was friendly to Bashar al-Assad at the outset of the conflict, and provided him with cover in the councils of NATO and in dealings with the Obama administration. But Bashar tested the patience and the indulgence of Prime Minister Recep Tayyip Erdogan. There were the flow of Syrian refugees into Turkey and the growing violations of religious sensibilities in Damascus—the attacks on mosques and preachers, the flagrant disregard for the pieties of devout Muslims. The party in power in Turkey was neo-Ottomanist and Sunni in its fidelity. It could not afford an open alliance with an Alawite Syrian ruler who had taken the plunge into a sectarian conflict. No wonder the hesitancy in official Turkish conduct. This hesitancy had fed the speculation—was it wishful thinking?—that the Turks could at any time opt for a military strike against the Syrian regime. This was too good to be true: deliverance at the hands of a Muslim neighbor, a NATO power with muscle, but a Muslim power still. The Turks were shrewd, they kept their options open, they would contest Iran's influence in Syria, but they would not step into the Syrian quagmire.

The policy in Ankara would evolve and come to reflect the rise of Prime Minister Erdogan as a political player of great consequence in Arab affairs. Erdogan had responded to the vacuum of power in the Arab world, and to the felt need among Sunni Arabs for a balance to the power and the schemes of Iran. A shrewd and decisive man, Erdogan understood that he couldn't ride the tumult of the Arab Spring and be a friend of the Syrian dictator nearby at the same time. In public and to great pan-Arab enthusiasm, Erdogan had launched a full-scale attack on the alliance with Israel that had been a pillar of the old Kemalist regime and the military. In the Arab intellectual and political circles there was talk of Turkey's prime minister as the new sultan—a harking back to the Ottomanist system. These Arab lands in the throes of rebellion and in search of a new political way—Syria, Egypt, Libya, Tunisia—had once been Ottoman provinces. No one was resurrecting that old empire, but Erdogan was offering himself as a model, a believer—no beard, no turban—a Muslim prime minister of a secular state. Turkey was in the midst of an economic boom, its leaders brimming with pride that their country had become the fifteenth-largest economy in the world, and Erdogan would let the Arabs see for themselves the wisdom of his way. Bashar had become a burden and an embarrassment, and the Erdogan government would all but walk away from him.

In early September, with no end in sight to the Syrian terror, Erdogan said that he was no longer in contact with Bashar al-Assad and does not intend to resume any relationship with him. It was all broken now, and Erdogan's language was remarkable: "He who bases his regime on blood will be drowned in blood. Mr. Assad, when you were shelling your people in Latakia from gunboats, you claimed you were shelling terrorists. Leaders should base their rule on legitimacy. You and the people around you have reached the point of no return." In the past, Erdogan had rebuked Bashar's younger brother and enforcer, Maher, and denounced the cruelty of his deeds. Now Bashar was placed at arm's length. Iran and the competition with Iran must have been on Erdogan's mind, for the Iranian patrons of Bashar had themselves begun to hint that the Syrian regime was in need of reform and that official violence would not carry the day.

A week or so after this break with Bashar, Erdogan would embark on nothing less than a victory lap through the three countries that had banished their rulers in the course of this Arab Spring—Egypt, Tunisia, Libya. He exuded confidence and optimism and indentified himself and his country with these rebellions. An entourage of businessmen and investors accompanied him. In Cairo, there was an adoring crowd for the successful Muslim "brother" who turned his back on Israel and chose them instead. He startled the Islamists when he described himself as a Muslim prime minister of a secular state. This wasn't what they expected, but he was sure that the Turkish path was the way out for the Arabs. He couldn't have made that run as the Syrian tyrant's friend. He bore the Arabs news of a new kind of political order—one that emerges out of the ballot box and is sustained economically by a devout bourgeoisie. There were skeptical Arabs, including those who remembered the Erdogan intimacy with Assad and the big role that Turkish companies played in the economy of Libya under Qaddafi. Moreover, those with a precise grasp of the political shifts of the region could recall that Turkey had done its best to thwart the NATO mission in Libya. But Erdogan had pulled it off. He had positioned his country on the side of the angels.

Time, and a scent for the mood of the Arab world he had ventured into, had sharpened Erdogan's message. On September 22, in a speech before the United Nations General Assembly, he situated his Syrian policy in the big changes sweeping the region. "The map of the Middle East is changing," he said. "From the beginning of these events we asked the governments to listen to their people. Countless times we asked the Syrian government to do so. We are neighbors and friends, we share a long border of 990 kilometers, there are blood ties between our two peoples. Friends tell the truth even if it is bitter." He had rendered advice to the Syrian rulers, but they had not listened. "Every drop of blood shed in Syria only widens the gap between the government and the people."

Several weeks later, Erdogan, in his most pointed language on Syria, said Bashar's behavior was the inheritance his father bequeathed him, "the cruelty that was a response to people in Hama, Homs, and Deraa." The Syrian people will be vindicated, he said, "rewarded for their glorious resistance." The Syrian regime was shaken by this rupture in Turkey's behavior. But in keeping with its displays of defiance, it insisted that it will not bend to Erdogan's pressure. "Whoever throws a flower at us, we will throw a flower back at him," Bashar's foreign minister said of the Turkish pressure. There was bluster there, but some truth as well. The Syrians and the Turks know each other quite well, their intelligence services having worked together in collusion and in enmity. In times of antagonism, the Syrians had sponsored Kurdish elements drawn from the extremist PKK, facilitated their entry into Turkey, and provided them sanctuary. The Syrians wanted it understood that they still had assets to bring into this contest.

States are cold, unsentimental monsters, and the Syrians were on guard when it came to the conduct of the Turkish state and its

Islamist leaders. The mysterious disappearance on Turkish soil of an army defector, Lt. Col. Hussein Harmoush, at the end of August served notice on the Syrian oppositionists that all was not well in Turkey, that they were at the mercy of their hosts. Harmoush had defected and made a video in June, calling on army officers and soldiers to mutiny against the regime. His relatively high rank had given heart that other defections would follow, and that a free Syrian army would come together. He was with his wife and children in Turkey, in a refugee camp in the province of Hatay under Turkish protection. On August 29, he would tell his wife that he was headed to a meeting with a man from the Turkish intelligence services. His cell phone went dead, and his wife was unable to contact him. Two weeks later, Harmoush turned up on Syrian television. He belittled the opposition. They had deluded him with promises of help, and the help had not materialized. He denied receiving orders to shoot protesters, and reading from the regime's script, he accused the Muslim Brotherhood of smuggling guns and terrorists into the country.

After this television appearance, he was not seen or heard from again. The Syrian opposition would draw its own conclusions: Turkish authorities had turned him over to Damascus. Press as they did the Turks, they could never get an answer as to what had transpired in this affair. Prime Minister Erdogan dodged the inquiries. The matter will be clarified, he said, and Turkish security would be cleared of suspicion of complicity in this matter. In the refugee camp that had been his sanctuary, his wife, Gofran Hejazi, an articulate woman, said that she did not know whether she was a wife or a widow. She told of his frustrations in the army and said that the senior commanders, all Alawis, had blocked his promotion. She knew the rules of this terrible war. She didn't think that people came out alive from the torture chambers of the regime. She feared him lost and held onto the consolation that paradise would be his abode. The traffic between the rulers in Ankara and their counterparts in Damascus was opaque to the Syrian oppositionists. Turkey could host opposition conferences, but the tale of Hussein Harmoush was a reminder to the oppositionists that they were up against a regime in Damascus steeped in the dirty tricks that states play.

Iraq presented the oddest of spectacles among Syria's neighbors. During Iraq's years of vulnerability (2003–2008), Syria had been a menace to the new order in Baghdad. In 2003, the regime had its highest religious authority, Mufti Ahmad Kuftaro, declare "jihad" against the Americans in Iraq, an obligation binding on all Muslims. The Syria-Iraq border was the passage of choice for Arab jihadists keen on warring against the Americans—and the Shia. It was in Syria where remnants of the Iraqi Baath and determined enemies of the new Iraq had made their home. Saddam's most notorious lieutenant, Izzat Ibrahim al-Douri (the King of Clubs in the deck of cards of the most-wanted Iraqi officials), operated out of Syria after the fall of his master's regime. He had huge amounts of cash and well over three decades of traffic with the House of Assad and its operatives. He had been engaged in illicit trade with members of the Assad family itself. He was now the leader of the Baath insurgency, with his friends and political standing providing him access and cover. To the "dead enders" and remnants of the Baath warring against the American project, al-Douri was a link to the dominion of old. Like his leader, al-Douri had been a foe of the Islamists. But on the run he made common cause with the jihadists, and his pronouncements became the standard mixture of religion and politics, of war against the "infidels" and their collaborators. He was not the only fugitive that the Iraqi rulers had to worry about. There was Mishan Jaburi, a former member of the new Iraqi parliament who had been stripped of his immunity on charges of corruption and had made his way to Damascus, where he launched a television station that glorified the jihadist war in Iraq. Jaburi had a Syrian wife and ample funds. His television station broadcast videos of insurgent attacks on American forces, and the Syrians had let him be. (A new station of his, Al-Rai, was still active in 2011. It was the last outlet that Muammar el-Qaddafi used for his calls to war against the new Libya and for his bombastic threats of turning his country into a "volcano of lava and fire.")

Beyond these figures of note and the Baathists dreaming of restoration and revenge, there was commerce to be had for the Syrian middlemen who escorted these jihadists from the Damascus airport to the border with Iraq. And there was a deliberate policy aimed at thwarting the American war and keeping the Americans and Iraqis busy with a bloody insurgency. The new rulers in Baghdad, struggling for a footing, had a world of resentments against the Damascus regime. On the face of it, the fledgling democracy in Baghdad should have thrown its support behind the Syrian opposition. But a different policy was playing out: the Shia-led government of Prime Minister Nuri al-Maliki was openly on the side of the Syrian rulers. In a stunning display of blatant willfulness, Nuri al-Maliki called on the Syrian opposition to take up the democratic path and participate in their country's elections. Maliki had spent seventeen years in Syria, an exile on the run from the regime of Saddam Hussein. He was an operative of a militant underground Shia movement, the Dawaa Party. He had opted for Syria because he had not taken to Iran; he quit that country after a sojourn of several years.

The Maliki years in Syria go a long way in explaining the riddle of Iraq's behavior in the face of the Syrian rebellion. When other Arab states were downgrading their relations with Syria—Saudi Arabia, Kuwait, and Bahrain had withdrawn their ambassadors from Damascus by August—Iraq was moving in the opposite direction. It was offering the Damascus regime moral support and signing trade deals with the embattled regime. An able Iraqi author and researcher, Nibras Kazimi has supplied an illuminating analysis of Maliki's outlook on the struggle for Syria. To begin, the long years in Syria would have required protection and funding from Maliki's hosts. These couldn't have been brilliant years for Iraqis at odds with Saddam Hussein. There was little hope that the Saddam tyranny could be overthrown. The Syrians would have seen the Iraqi exiles as a side bet, a way of harassing the Saddam regime. While in Syria, Kazimi tells us, Nuri al-Maliki had lived in a modest Shia neighborhood of Damascus. He was there during the terrible bloodletting between the Alawi minority and the Muslim Brotherhood. He witnessed the gunning down of Alawi professionals for no other reason than their religious affiliation. He was a sectarian—this can't be denied, his Shia self-identification ran deep—and the Syrian years strengthened his belief in the power of the Sunni-Shia schism. The view that the Iraqi tilt to Syria is a tribute to Iran is, at best, a partial truth. This was a deliberate Iraqi policy that drew its power from the outlook of Prime Minister Maliki and those around him.

Maliki was convinced that the victory of the rebellion in Syria would mean the advent of a Sunni-fundamentalist regime on Iraq's western border. He was not a satrap of Iran. He always had a dark view of the Persian theocracy, but he saw in the regime in Syria, and in Hezbollah in Beirut, a hedge against the Sunni pact of Saudi Arabia, Jordan, Egypt, and the smaller monarchies in the Gulf. The Saudis had opposed the emergence of this Iraq mid-wifed by American power. They had never taken to Maliki, and now in power in a big Arab capital, he was keen to contest their will. In the Sunni world, it had been nearly impossible to find any sympathy for the coming of age of the Iraqi Shia, and Maliki himself was seen as a man driven by his Shia fidelity. There had been that phantom of a "Shia crescent" stretching from Iran to Lebanon, through Iraq and Syria. The Jordanian ruler, Abdullah II, was fond of this image. He peddled it to the Americans in the hope of enlisting American funding and help, giving Jordan and its security forces a role in containing this Shia menace. So was Hosni Mubarak, with his country safe and removed from the Sunni-Shia fault line. It was his belief that the Shia Arabs were loyal to Iran rather than to their governments. He saw whole communities in Bahrain, Iraq, and Lebanon as a fifth column of the Persian state. This was the Egyptian ruler's way of staking claim to the treasure of the Sunni monarchies and principalities of the Arabian Penin-sula and the Persian Gulf. Now that Maliki had given ammunition to that view, he saw nothing in Syria save a struggle between an Alawi regime and a Sunni opposition.

Around Maliki there was a new political class. I had been given access to them in extended visits to Iraq over the course of several years. They were not a terribly worldly breed. They had limited education and horizons. They had grown up on a diet of Shia martyrology, they had always been outsiders, and they had led marginal lives in Damascus, London, or Tehran through the long decades of Sunni rule in their country. So many of them had known the official cruelty of the Saddam dictatorship and lost loved ones and family members to the terror. As in the Shia tales of loss and deliverance, an American-led war and the weight of

Shia demography had given them political primacy. They were keen on a settlement of an overdue historical account. To this political class—as it is to the Shia operatives in Lebanon—Damascus and the cities of Homs and Hama were fortresses of Sunni Islam, repositories of a worldview that had always been contemptuous of the Shia. Damascus had been the seat of the Umayyad Empire. It was in that city that the disinheritance of the Shia had begun, in the middle years of the seventh century. It was to Damascus, the chronicles maintain, that the severed head of the iconic Shia martyr, Imam Hussein, had been brought, to the ruler's palace, after the tragedy of Karbala in southern Iraq in the year 680. The Sunnis of Damascus had never acknowledged the horror of the deed, and the Shia had never forgotten it. This rebellion—with new technology, posted on YouTube, captured by telephone cameras, and expressed in the language of democracy and civil rights—would be seen through an old prism. Maliki and the newly empowered Shia political class in Baghdad couldn't release themselves from history's grip. They were convinced that the Syrian rebellion, well-intentioned at the beginning, had been hijacked by Salafists recruited and financed by Saudi Arabia. Al Jazeera television gave sustenance to the rebels, and that, too, was seen as part of a wider Sunni attempt to tip the scales of power in the region. Al Jazeera had been no friend of the Shia of Iraq in their struggle with the jihadists. Its enthusiasm for the Syrian rebellion was evidence that the old lines of conflict in the region around them had not altered.

THE ACCOUNT between the regime and the people of Hama had a truth of its own. After the bloodletting of 1979–1982, the regime had let Hama be, and the Hamawis turned inward in sullen recognition of their weakness. Historically, they had looked to Damascus and provisioned its caravans. Their politics were an extension of Damascene sensibilities and preference. But Damascus had hardly stirred during their ordeal. Now Hama was permitted its silent hatred of the rulers. In the late 1980s Charles Glass, an intrepid writer traveling from Alexandretta to Aqaba for his book, *Tribes With Flags*, visited Hama. About six years or so after the events, he could still discern the presence of what had happened here. There had been celebrated "Hama prints," white cotton linens used for tablecloths, bedspreads, and the like. Whole families did that sort of work, their craft handed down from one generation to the next. When he queried why there were so few Hama prints in the souk, a shopkeeper was reluctant to provide a full answer. There had been families, he said, that had done that kind of work, and they could be seen drying the cloths by the river. This was "before 1982," the man said. "Now, only one family is left."

"Tons of rubble" were still there in the souk, Glass wrote, an open area which had been a busy marketplace was battered, the rubble pushed to the extremities. The traveler had been making his way through Syria, and here in Hama there was something missing—something that he encountered everywhere else in Syria. "In all of Hama's shops, offices, squares, and souks, indoors or out, there was not a single photograph, painting, or statue of President Hafez al-Assad." In a quiet government library, he came upon the only portrait of the ruler he would see in Hama. It was the familiar countenance of the man, but the artist had added a touch; he had "placed in the president's hands a set of worry beads." A small attempt to render him more familiar, less menacing.

When the rebellion of 2011 arrived in Hama, the protagonists picked up an old thread. The blood feud had not been settled. Alawis with a taste for tales of old hurts speak of a time when it was perilous for Alawi villagers to venture into the warrens of Hama. They tell of beatings and killings at the hands of the enforcers and the agents of the landed families. Now the Hamawis had woes of their own to narrate.

CHAPTER SEVEN

The Truth of the Sects

PANDORA'S BOX had been opened, and out of it had sprung that rancid sectarianism of the Arab east—its Sunni-Shia fault line. This, after all is said and done, accounts for that peculiar Iraqi attitude toward the Syrian revolt. A man of the Iraqi political class, shrewd and something of a gadfly, explained to me the reason he had not celebrated the rebellion next door. He was no friend of autocracy. He had fought and agitated against Saddam Hussein and basked in the messy freedom of Iraq. He had gone to Syria, he told me, and even visited the city of Hama. He had not liked what he had seen. There was a noble rebellion, genuine in its opposition to dictatorship, he said, but the die-hards and the Salafists had pulled the rug from underneath it. There was a rhythmic chant that made an impression on him, *al-Alawi ala taboot, wa al-Masihi ala Beirut* (the Alawi in the coffin, and the Christian to Beirut). Hard-core elements, jihadists who had battled the Americans in Iraq, and Sunni Iraqis from the Anbar had joined this fight against the Syrian government, he said. The minorities—Alawis, Christians—had a lot to fear from this rebellion. What hope he had was that Bashar himself would rise above the Baath Party—in a note of irony given the loaded history of the term in his own country, his preference was for the de-Baathification of the Syrian regime. The secular claims of the "folks in Deraa and Homs and

111

Hama" were not credible to this man. There was a lot in Syrian culture he admired—its secularism, its openness—and he did not want to see it replaced by Sunni rule. There were emancipated women in the streets and a vibrant social life. The Salafists would lay all this to waste, he believed. He acknowledged the peculiarity of an Alawi regime in a majority Sunni country. It was against the natural order of things, he said. He didn't think the Alawis had used their decades in power well. But he could not embrace the sort of regime the rebellion might give rise to.

The sectarianism stalking the Syrian rebellion was bound to spill into Lebanon with even greater force than could be felt in Iraq. The unadorned truth of the sectarian implications of what was playing out in Syria were laid bare by a supremely political priest of the Maronite Church, Patriarch Bishara al-Rai. The newly installed patriarch was visiting Paris in early September when he voiced the sort of sentiment that is whispered in private, but rarely uttered by someone of his stature. The Syrian regime was in the process of reform and needed and deserved room to maneuver, he said. Bashar was a man who needed time to bring about change; the Syrian ruler could not "work miracles." Were the opposition to Bashar to prevail, the Sunnis of Syria would unite with their brothers in Lebanon and undo Lebanon's balance. The Christians of the east were in jeopardy, and the patriarch harked back to the fate of the Christians of Iraq: they hadn't fared well under the new order, and the same fate lay in store for the Christians in Syria. The Damascus regime had always claimed that its rule provided a shield for the minorities. Now the leader of the Maronite Church had come out to give it backing—and in Paris of all places. French President Sarkozy had become a fierce critic of the Assad regime, and he was to tell the patriarch that the regime of Bashar was done and incapable of reform.

The patriarch returned home to a mighty storm. The Maronite Church is a national church. Its creed is attachment to Lebanon and its independence. The founding ethos of the Maronites is their migration from the Syrian plains to the freedom and "purity" of their home in Mount Lebanon. The sentiments of the patriarch were veritable heresy. Bishara al-Rai's predecessor, Cardinal Nasrallah Sfeir, had been heroic and steadfast in his resistance to Syria's steady encroachment on Lebanon. He had fought the Syrians when practically all of Lebanon's leading figures had given in. He had been true to his church's mission. Earlier in 2011, he had stepped aside in an unusual turn in the affairs of his church. It was no secret that he was at odds with a fellow Maronite, former General Michel Aoun, now a power in the Lebanese Parliament and an ally of Syria and Hezbollah. (Aoun was an acrobat, true to the self-defeating ways of the Lebanese political class. He had once been a fervent enemy of Syria, but after fifteen years in exile in France, he had made an abrupt shift and now rode with Hezbollah and Damascus.) Sfeir had understood the balance of forces around him, and there were reports that the Vatican had thrown its weight behind a change at the helm of the church. It wanted a clerical leader who could strike a bargain with the Shia in Lebanon and, by extension, the Alawis in Damascus. It was true Sfeir led a divided church, but this had been an essential feature in Maronite life.

The new patriarch—beardless, in love with the limelight and press conferences, dubbed "the omnipatriarch"—had given sustenance to the regime in Damascus at a time of fearsome repression in Syria. Lebanon was still a country given to political arguments, and the patriarch was not spared. He was a troublesome political priest, said Michael Young, an outspoken Lebanese-American columnist for Beirut's English-language paper, *The Daily Star.*

Young was unsparing: "For believers, and even unbelievers, a
church that sustains a butcher is a contradiction. What kind of
sordid religious establishment is it that takes the side of a despot
against his own people? How can Rai pontificate about Christian
love and communion, then with a straight face warn of the potential dangers if the Assads are removed? Rai mentioned the fate of
Iraq's Christians as a path to be avoided by Maronites. Unfortu-
nately that community is suffering today because it was indentified with Saddam Hussein's brutality. Is that the outcome Rai
seeks for Syria's Christians, or Lebanon's?"

Closer to the fire, Michel Kilo, a prominent figure of the
Syrian opposition and a Christian born in the coastal town of
Latakia, came forth with a detailed rejection of the patriarch's
message. Kilo brought authenticity to this sensitive debate. A
prolific journalist and commentator, Kilo had done stints in
prison for his politics. In 2006, he had been sentenced to three
years in prison on charges of "weakening national sentiment and
encouraging sectarian strife." His trademark fearlessness was on
full display as he addressed his "Beatitude the Maronite Patriarch
as a man of politics rather than a man of religion." The patriarch,
Kilo wrote, had spoken "in the name of the Christians of the
East, even though he represents a minority of them, and the rest
of the Eastern Christians never asked him to be their spokesman." A bitter struggle raged in Syria, and "a politician, let alone
a cleric," would have been more careful in his utterances. The
patriarch had inserted himself into the Sunni-Shia conflict,
"though, what is happening in Syria is the playing out of a different kind of conflict." A war rages between "totalitarian regimes"
and their populations; the regimes have nothing to offer save pain
and deprivation. A messy conflict was raging in Lebanon, and
the Maronites themselves divided into two opposing camps—one

with Hezbollah and Syria, the other with a broad Sunni-led coalition—and the patriarch should have tread carefully. "There's no need to affirm that al-Rai's political stances are incorrect. He needs to be reminded of a statement by Hegel, who said that freedom emerged in the history of mankind with Christianity. I remind him of this quote because his position as head of the Maronite Church binds him to have faith in it and act according to its content."

There were two ways the minorities could go, the flood of commentaries noted: the shield of the secular dictatorship, or the risks and rewards of democratic politics. The patriarch ducked for cover, but the issue he opened up would not go away. From neighboring Syria the evidence pointed to the unease of the Christians: they had the ruler's protection, but they could not be sure of the costs of the dictatorship's embrace. Bashar had paid no tribute to subtlety: in the midst of this rebellion he was to remove his Alawi defense minister and replace him with a Christian. The minorities were being summoned for a stand against the Sunni wave.

In Damascus, the patriarch of the Greek Orthodox Church, Ignace IV, had let it be known that the regime was preferable to the sort of order that might emerge out of the upheaval. This Arab Spring was being Islamized, and Christian Arabs were living atop a volcano: they had no brilliant option. There were no Western gunboats, and there was no consular protection as had been the case in the age of empire. Gone were the days when France, Russia, England, Germany, and the Protestant missions lent them their coattails. Their crisis was made sharper still by the evasions of political language all around them. The Christians had bet on Arab nationalism, but it had failed them as it was Islamized from below. The regime insisted that its authority was needed against the fundamentalists, and the opposition was equally sure of its own secular leanings. Arabs hadn't been truthful about their religious and sectarian differences, and Greater Syria itself had been a land of feuding communities and identities. Secular nationalism had denied and papered over these deeply held attachments and rivalries, but the fight in Syria, as in Lebanon for a good generation prior to that, had brought these rivalries out into the open.

"I haven't yet come across one spark of national feeling: it is all sects and hatreds and religions," Freya Stark wrote in 1928 in a letter from Syria. Edward Atiyah, a noted Christian Arab man of letters, wrote in a similar vein in *An Arab Tells His Story: A Study of Loyalties*, in 1946: "If ever there was a country in which every conceivable influence, divine and mundane, physical and moral, inherent and extraneous, militated against national unity and the formation of patriotic sentiment, that country was Syria before 1914." These fault lines of sect and community had not gone away, and that world in Greater Syria—Syria and Lebanon, to be precise—had not found a way out of the hold of sectarianism. The dreaded Assad boys—Bashar and younger brother Maher— were both married to Sunnis. It was said that their father had claimed on the occasion of his mother's death that he and his family were Sunnis and that a Sunni cleric would lead the prayer during her ceremony of farewell. But in a moment of peril, the call of the sect trumped the claims of secularism.

At the heart of this fight for Syria was nothing less than the ability of Sunni Islam to hold its own against the "compact communities" and the rival sects. The Alawis had upended Sunni rule in Damascus, and Beirut had all but slipped under the control of the Shia stepchildren, countryside folks who had descended on Beirut from the Bekaa Valley and the southern hinterland. In

May 2008, in a traumatic moment for the Sunnis of Beirut, Hezbollah had made short shrift of a Sunni militia. Its fighters overran the Sunni positions with great ease. Tripoli, a coastal city that straddles the Syria-Lebanon border, was a fortress of Sunni Islam with an Alawi minority that Syrian rule had aided and emboldened. It was riddled with this new, poisonous sectarian schism. Tripoli had never taken to its inclusion within the borders of Lebanon, which had been forced by French rule. Its ties to the city of Homs, across the border, were of greater meaning and import to its people than its bonds with Beirut and Mount Lebanon. Its animating passion, in the 1950s and the 1960s, was Arab nationalism. With the eclipse of that movement, Tripoli fell for a new calling: the jihad, political Islam, the anxiety of a conservative Sunni society over the increasing power of the minorities. Syria played a double-game with the jihadists: it infiltrated their ranks, and it used them for its own purposes but never trusted them. All the while, Alawi power grew in the shadow of the Syrian presence. There were approximately 120,000 Alawis in the country, and the overwhelming majority of them inhabited Tripoli. They had a neighborhood of their own, Jebel Mohsen, and they were passionately committed to the Damascus regime and fearful of the consequences were that regime to fall. They were mobilized and armed to check the power of the Islamists. The Syrian regime, with a quiescent Lebanese government doing its bidding, granted the Alawis two seats in the Lebanese Parliament. Lebanon's naturalization laws had been subverted, as Syrian Alawis who had migrated across the border were given coveted Lebanese citizenship.

As the ground burned in Syria and the power of the Shia movement Hezbollah grew in Beirut, Sunni Tripoli bristled: the schismatics were gaining the upper hand, and the pure faith of

Sunni Islam was endangered. Under the cover of "resistance" to Israel, Hezbollah had become an army in its own right, perhaps superior in firepower to Lebanon's national army. And across the border from Tripoli, the good sons of Hama and Homs were fighting for their lives against a godless, tyrannical regime that feigned militancy against Israel while carrying out a fearsome crackdown against the Sunni population. Sunni Islam was being tested where it mattered—on the battlefield. It was not faring well. During the Ottoman centuries, the Sunni communities of Beirut and Tripoli in today's Lebanon, and Homs, Hama, Damascus, and Aleppo in Syria had been ascendant, and their "notables" were the pillars of public order. National independence was a starting gun for all concerned—the Sunnis, the compact communities, and the minorities. The initial advantage had gone to the Sunnis, but time and Shia demography in Lebanon and the rule of the gun and the military in Syria had altered the balance, and the Sunnis were thrown on the defensive. They were dubbed *yatama al-sultan* (the sultan's orphans).

Instinctively, the Sunnis in Syria and Lebanon looked to each other for support, and they did their best to pull big and influential Sunni players—Egypt, Saudi Arabia—into their midst. The self-confidence they exuded through the 1950s and 1960s concealed a nervousness about their hold on power. They had taught Arab nationalism to the Alawis in Syria and the Shia in Lebanon. Now these communities had been empowered by these very same ideologies. Urbanization had done its work as well, as Alawis from the mountains made their way to Damascus and as the Shia of the Bekka Valley and southern Lebanon swamped Beirut. Big regional changes were making themselves felt. Egypt had long pulled back from the Fertile Crescent, while Shia Iran came bearing militancy, guns, and money. The Saudis were doing their best

to balance these forces, but they and the funds they provided were
no match for the changes on the ground.

An enterprising reporter for the Lebanese daily *An-Nahar*,
Radwan Aqeel was able to convey the wrath of Tripoli and its
sense of solidarity with the rebellion next door. In early August,
about four months into Syria's troubles, nothing was hidden as the
reporter witnessed street protests and made his way into the city's
mosques and the homes of its Salafi leaders. An Iranian flag was
burned and had been placed alongside an Israeli flag. One activist
told the reporter that remote Australia was closer to him than the
Shia slums of southern Beirut, a stronghold of Hezbollah. Those
Hezbollah weapons of the "resistance" given sanctity and protection in the name of fighting Israel were the weapons of "heretics,"
this man said. It is the duty of every Muslim to come to the aid of
brothers in distress, and Tripoli owed its loyalty to Muslims in
Syria fighting a merciless tyrant. Tripoli was home to an influential
Salafi preacher, Zakaria al-Masri, who was an imam and prayer
leader of the Hamza Mosque. The reporter called on him and
talked to him in his library, which was a "forest" of books and
leaflets. Support for Syria's Sunnis, Masri observed, was obligatory
and part of "commanding right and forbidding wrong" in Islam.
The Damascus regime was killing Sunnis, pure and simple, and
the believers in Tripoli could not stand idly by. He was offended
that Hezbollah—and its operatives, supporters, and well-funded
television station—had rallied to the support of far-off Shia in
Bahrain, while Tripoli had been unable, or disallowed, to rise in
defense of Syria's embattled people.

Iran and Israel are two sides of the same coin, the militant
preacher opined. Iran, an allegedly Islamic republic, is a state that
deviates from the rule of Islam. The believers should not be hood-
winked into supporting Hezbollah's leader, Hassan Nasrallah.

"Should we love and support Hassan Nasrallah merely because he fights Israel, or claims to do so? That would be akin to loving Hitler because he was an enemy of the Jews. Nasrallah's sole aim is to protect the Persian state and spread its influence. The Shia doctrine is a danger to the Arabs, and the sooner the Arabs understand this, the better." Masri had no interest in a dialogue with Nasrallah, and he neither had a Shia friend nor wanted one. In his view, the Shia were *kuffar* (heretics and apostates), and the Alawis were a step beyond still, infidels with no claim on Islam.

There was no conciliating Tripoli to the order of power in Damascus—or in Beirut. Najib Mikati, a son of Tripoli and a telecommunications magnate, was prime minister in Beirut. He had come into that office through the grace of Hezbollah and Syria. His foreign minister, a Shia, had been ambassador to Iran. Mikati had been elected to parliament from Tripoli. But most of Tripoli's population now disowned him. It was the holy month of Ramadan (which overlapped this year with the month of August), and Mikati, as befitting a man of means, had been providing the poor with *iftar* dinners to break the fast. His offering was boycotted, for Tripoli's mainstream—let alone the Salafists and their preachers—this wealthy son of the city had broken with his own.

In our perception, the Levant was supposed to be a place that knew how to split differences. This new sectarianism was of a wholly different nature, and the differences could not be papered over. The Syrian opposition to the regime had done its best to claim that this rebellion presented no threat to the Alawis and the other minorities. One day of protest, a Friday, was named in honor of a figure of old, Shaykh Salih al-Ali, an Alawite notable who had fought against the French in 1920. He had resisted the intrusion of the French into the Alawite heartland and died in 1926, in the seclusion of the Alawite mountain. Very few if any young Syrians knew of his exploits, but the tribute to him was meant to reassure the Alawis that they had a place in the rebellion against the Assads. The tribute could do no harm, but even Shaykh Salih al-Ali was an ambiguous figure. Nationalist historiography claimed him as a son of Syria who rose in rebellion against colonial rule. But in the Alawi mountain, they knew better. They remembered him as a kinsman who fought for the autonomy of the Alawites and had been dubious of the politics of the urban elite and their nationalist pretensions.

Were the vigilantes of the regime, the *shabiha* (ghosts), roaming the cities in their black attire Alawi young men given their writ by the regime and let loose on the protesters, or were they just goons and hired bullies? There must have been in their ranks opportunists drawn from every community, even good Sunni boys out for pay and rewards in a country with shrinking economic possibilities. This must have been a phenomenon akin to Fedayeen Saddam, the vigilantes and thugs of Saddam Hussein who drew on Sunnis and Shiites alike. Still, the prevailing and safe assumption was that these shabiha were newly urbanized Alawis from the countryside doing the regime's dirty work. On September 23, a YouTube video post by Al Jazeera, offered me a confirmation of the sectarianism of this terrible time. Shot on the outskirts of Homs, it was one of the "trophy videos" that security forces and men of the shabiha take as they torment their prey. These videos find their way to the black market and are usually sold by the perpetrators themselves. In this video, Louay Amer, a bearded young man wearing a white thoub, is in the hands of a group of "special forces," who are recognizable by their red armbands. He is being beaten with a cane on the soles of his feet. He is toyed with. "Take my picture with him," one of the soldiers says to the cameraman as he grabs his victim's beard. "Take my picture with him." Louay

Amer is pleading for mercy, and his tormentors want him to offer tribute to Bashar. He provides it, the sad tribute offered to leaders in this sad Arab time. "With our blood and our souls, we sacrifice ourselves for you Bashar," the man proclaims. Louder, his captors demand. He does so, while the caning goes on. Soldiers are kicking him in the head and stomping on his chest. Liar, they say, dismissing his profession of loyalty to Bashar.

There is a Sunni cleric, Shaykh Adnan al-Arour, a militant who was born in Hama but based in Saudi Arabia. He was something of a presence on television, and he had been zealous in his opposition to the Syrian regime. To the Alawis, Arour was evil incarnate. The men of the special forces are taunting their captive: Arour could do nothing for him now, could he?

This display of brutality does not end well. A second posting shows the man's corpse with signs of torture all over his face. Louay Amer worked in Saudi Arabia, he had savings, and he had the beard and the white thoub. Would a Sunni band of vigilantes have shown him the same cruelty and contempt? We can't provide a sure answer, for men and women in cruel times and places go at it with abandon. But the posting conveys the unmistakable impression of a sectarian vendetta. Louay Amer's tormentors knew that they were going to kill him; the caning and the taunts were thrown in for an additional measure of brutality and humiliation. No proclamation by decent oppositionists gathered in Istanbul or Brussels, affirming the unity of all Syrians, could dispense with the sectarian hatred.

THE DOORS WERE NEVER SHUT in the face of the Alawis. The opposition insisted that the "esteemed community," *al-taifa*

al-karima, was innocent of the crimes of the House of Assad. Any cracks in the Alawi edifice were seized upon as evidence that the national idea survives. When three Alawi men of religion from the city of Homs—their stature unknown—spoke in opposition to the regime, their breaking ranks was hailed as proof that deliverance was near and that the Alawis were destined to break with the rulers. But the rupture never came, as the Alawis were invested in the regime and captured by it. They had nowhere to go. This regime had pulled them out of rural poverty and persecution, brought them power and dividends, and now landed them in supreme peril. It took less than five decades for the sons of peasants to rise to the apex of power. The regime had made it a punishable crime to describe political life in sectarian terms, but the truth was mightier than official edicts.

The most honest assessment by an Alawi of the predicament of his people was made in June 2011, on the *Syria Comment* site, by a writer using the pseudonym Khudr. The essay, "The Alawi Dilemma Revisited," has the sort of honesty missing in both the regime's evasions and the opposition's wishful thinking. Khudr went to the heart of things: there is no such thing, he wrote, as a nonpracticing Alawi. One is born into the faith. The Alawis have very few religious books, five in total, to instruct them about their faith. "Our identity is centered on our culture, the coastal accent, the special celebrations, the habits. We have nothing in common: we are united by our common sense of injustice over the past centuries. Many will argue that the statute of limitations has run out on our sense of persecution, particularly as Alawis have dominated Syria's security state for almost fifty years." Khudr lays out the oddity of it, a sense of persecution animating a ruling community. That sense of persecution, he writes, is "alive and well in our collective psyche." In the past the Alawis had been forced to dissimulate, and it was the regime that had given them their solidarity. "The only meeting ground or assembly point for Alawis, where we didn't have to pretend that we were something we weren't, was deep in the inner sanctum of the security state. We found ourselves in the clubby security of the secret services, the army officer academies, and the worker and agricultural syndicates in the coastal areas. These were all regime sanctioned and established institutions that linked our identity to the security state and Assad rule. We haven't much history—at least not that we have documented. We have been too busy pretending that we are no different from the Muslims to build our community identity. We don't even know much about our religion to grasp onto. Alawis have defined themselves over the last 40 years as the rulers of Syria, and not much else."

Former opponents of the Assad regime, he added, are turning into "Basharists" now that the regime is under attack. Nor was the Alawi dilemma in Syria comparable to that of the Sunnis of Iraq under Saddam. The Sunnis, the ruling minority in Iraq, belonged to Islam's and the Arab world's dominant community. They had primacy among the Arabs in "countries stretching from Morocco to Saudi Arabia." The Alawis lack that sense of confidence and belonging, Khudr added. They will have "to fight to the end" and stay with the Assads, doubts and all. It is not a pretty future that the Alawis contemplate as their dominion offers them no safety, this immensely thoughtful writer concludes.

It would be no easy matter speaking to this insoluble crisis of the Alawites. On September 12, in Cairo, the Syrian opposition gave it a try. A conference was held under the banner of national unity. An open appeal was made to the Alawites. Confessionalism was a crime, the organizers of this conference proclaimed, hence the importance of preserving national unity. There were

Islamists within the ranks of this assembly, indeed they drove its agenda. For what it was worth, this gathering insisted that it did not view the regime as the rule of a "particular community" but as the dominion of those who were willing tools and beneficiaries of the dynasty in power. Nor had this regime, these oppositionists said, favored any particular sect. It had oppressed all, and had reserved for any Alawites who challenged it a punishment more draconian than it meted out to others. The shadow of the sectarian troubles of the 1980s hovered over these proceedings, and those gathered here spoke of the past. There would be no sectarian deeds of revenge, they said, and no one would be "deemed guilty by virtue of their sectarian belonging."

Thomas Pierret, an able interpreter of Syrian Islam who had done extensive field research in the country, had it right: this was not likely to reassure the Alawites, but it was better than the furies that had played out in the 1980s. The theological position of the Alawites had not been resolved, and no assembly in Cairo could paper over the schism between the Alawis and mainstream, Sunni Islam. A great deal of effort on the part of the Alawites had gone into affirming that they were a community of Islam. This had backfired, for by the strictures of the faith, the Alawites were a sect that had begun as a schism within Islam and had ended up with its own doctrinal integrity, a faith apart. The call of this assembly in Cairo had the support of one figure of controversy, the incendiary Adnan al-Arour. The Sunni preacher had come to fame through a satellite TV channel, Al-Wisal, based in Saudi Arabia. Arour held out only fire and damnation for the Alawites. In a sermon delivered in May 2011, he had promised that no harm would come to Alawites "neutral" in this struggle, but the others would be shown no mercy and their bodies would be "thrown to the dogs." Alawite tyranny on one end, a violent fate on the other.

Syria laid bare, perhaps better than any other Arab land, the defect of the Arab postcolonial state. National integration had been a pretense, and the state itself was *ghanima* (war booty) conquered and kept by a ruling caste that hoards what the place has to offer. The young men—Greek Orthodox, Sunnis, Druze, Ismailis, and, yes, Alawis—who came together several decades earlier under the banners of the Baath had thought they would build something better than the order of the "feudalists," the merchants, and the men of religion. The first generation of Baathists had written their own obituaries of that early dream of political idealism. The shabiha, with their clubs and guns, had issued out of that willful innocence.

The oppositionists had to be given to a measure of optimism in the face of prohibitive odds. They waited for a split in the Alawi community. Ismael al-Khalidi, head of the "coalition of Syrian tribes," spoke in this vein to *Al Watan Al Arabi*, on September 30. The revolt will prevail within "two or three months," he said, the security services will not win, and the "Alawi family" will break with the regime to safeguard itself and avoid retribution against its members. The Alawis have not rebelled, he added, they were waiting for "guarantees" from the opposition, assurances that only those whose "hands are sullied with the blood of the Syrian people will be punished." The Alawis did not rule Syria, nor did the Baath, Khalidi said. The country was ruled by a gang of five men: Bashar, his brother Maher, and three of their maternal Makhlouf relatives, Mohamed, Hafez, and Rami.

This tribal leader, a Sunni, offered an affirmation, a truth that many Alawites had continued to proclaim. The Alawites as such did not rule Syria, but the rulers were Alawites. It was a distinction with a difference—a difference of great importance to the poor Alawites, urban and rural alike. But the difference was lost amid this increasingly sectarian fight. No one had a convincing script as to the fate of the Alawis. In the more apocalyptic scenarios, that community would make a run for it and return to the mountain villages which were its original home. This had been a charge hurled at the Alawis since their rise to power—that on a dark day when their power is broken they would return to the Jebel Ansariyah (the Alawi Mountain), and to the coastal plain at its foot. There were fresh rumors that the regime has already secured the access points to the Alawi heartland, from Jisr al-Shughour in the north to Tell Kalakh along the border with Lebanon. The mountains and villages behind the coastal city of Latakia, in the interwar years, had been home to nearly 90 percent of the Alawi population of Syria. In that secluded world, they had guarded and fought for their autonomy against the Ottomans, the French, and the urban elite who came to power in Damascus after independence. For those who love scripts of catastrophe, the Alawis would set Damascus and the plains ablaze as they retreated into their own world. "We have the mountain and the coast," a minor Alawi religious figure told the political journalist Nibras Kazimi in 2007. The man was a caretaker of an Alawi shrine high in the mountains. "We cannot live with them," he said of the Sunnis. Then came the fantasy. "Aleppo, Homs, and Hama were all Alawite cities, but they were all massacred." This was consolation, for the land and agriculture had long been annulled, and the men and women of the mountain had become citified and had grown attached to their new comforts. National integration may not have been a brilliant success, but no Alawi generals, businessmen, and professionals were pining for those villages of yesteryear. Old Man Assad was born in his ancestral village of Qardaha, and his children were creatures of Damascus.

The sectarianism was making itself felt with each passing day. On October 2, Sariya Hassoun, the 22-year-old son of the mufti of the republic, was struck down on the Aleppo-Idlib road. His

father, Ahmad Hassoun, was reviled by the oppositionists as a
man of the Sunni establishment who did the regime's bidding. In
one demonstration in Homs, the protesters had chanted: "Listen,
listen Hassoun, take off your turban and put on horns." This was
no single, isolated episode, and Mufti Hassoun was no friend of
this rebellion. He saw it as a wind stirred up by outsiders—
Saudis, Americans, you name it.

There is a tradition in Syria of the Sunni ulama keeping a
respectable distance from the Baath rulers lest they "burn their
wings" by too close an association with the state. The mufti had
long crossed that barrier. He was, the scholar Thomas Pierret
notes, the first non-Damascene occupant of the post since its cre-
ation in 1947, a political man with modest scholarly credentials.
He was no stranger to controversy and had been in the crosshairs
of the politico-religious opponents of the regime. In 2010, he was
widely quoted in a London-based Arabic daily as saying to a
group of American visitors engaged in an interfaith dialogue that
"if the Prophet Muhammad asked me to disbelieve in Christianity and Judaism, I would disbelieve in him, and if he ordered me
to kill people, I would tell him that he was not a prophet." A
coalition of religious conservatives in Damascus and anti-regime
elements from the Muslim Brotherhood had come together to
condemn him. An influential Salafi preacher living in exile in
London, Abu Basir al-Tartusi condemned the mufti as a "heretic"
and a "henchman" of the dictatorship. "You, Hassoun, are the
mufti of tyrants. You are the mufti of the sectarian Baathist
regime that is suppressing the Syrian people with iron and fire. I
would like to say to you: be prepared for your doom. Nobody
has dared to slander or insult the prophet without facing grave
punishment in this world and the hereafter." In an odd align-
ment, more liberal clerics and civil society activists had rallied to

the mufti's defense, but the damage had been done. This cruel assassination of his son was a reminder of the hazards of the deadly mix between religion and politics, all the more so in a time of ruinous passions and atavisms.

The mufti bade his son farewell in Aleppo with a moving eulogy that must stand, for me, as one of the most eloquent usages of the Arabic language I have ever encountered. It was played and replayed on Syrian television. It was posted on YouTube on October 3. A true master of the language, the mufti pulled off a rare performance. He spoke to and of his son as a bereaved father, and he appealed to his country's troubled people and to Arabs beyond. Grief and defiance alternated in his oration, the personal grief merged with the political meaning of the occasion. Speaking without notes, he told of a young man who was loving to his family and friends. He said to the departed son that his mother had found him a future bride just a day or so before his murder. The father knew that he himself was the target and wished he had been struck down instead. There had been the cruelties inflicted on the children of Deraa, and the mufti linked his grief with Deraa's: "I told the sons of Deraa your blood is our blood, your honor is our honor." He had raised Sariya to be a martyr in Palestine, instead he was killed by one of his own. "I beseech the families of the martyrs to say enough of the killing of the children of Syria. My son is now in God's mercy. But the messenger of God reminded us that the destruction of the holy Kaaba, stone by stone, is less offensive than the taking of one innocent soul."

The mufti was made to suffer this cruelest of deeds, but he was only a "bridge between the leader and the people," a servant of all of Syria's 23 million people. The target of this seditious time, he said, was not a specific regime or a specific ruler, but Syria itself, this "noble and blessed land" asked to kneel before its enemies.

There were members of his guild, Shaykh al-Azhar in Cairo and Shaykh Yusuf Qaradawi in Qatar, who had spoken out against the Assad regime. The mufti spoke directly to them, and reminded them that they, and his son alike, will stand in the presence of God on judgment day. *Ashab al-fatawa* (those who issue fatwas), he said, will be brought to account for what they had done. "Sariya, tell the messenger of God that the Arabs now have satellite channels and that Syria is their target. And *ashab al-internet* (the people of the Internet), they will come before God as well, the arbiter and the judge of us all." The bereaved father was a protagonist in this struggle, and he addressed the Arab rulers who sent "guns and money" to Syria and who withdrew their ambassadors. He called on them to come and see for themselves the peace and the safety of Syria's cities.

The mufti sought no vengeance: "To you who killed my son, I ask God that you are not forced to drink from the same cup of sorrow that I do, this cup of grief. I ask God to forgive you." He was a man of the state, and he offered his own reading of the man at the helm of the state. He spoke of him as a leader he knew well, a man who was not attached to the prerogatives of his office and who wanted to lead Syria to a safe harbor and then step aside. State patronage had raised the mufti—a son and a son-in-law of clerics before him—to his exalted position and he had come to considerable wealth, his detractors said of him, and now he was to know this shattering loss. It was a cathartic moment for Syria, but the lines were drawn and this father's grief was helpless in the face of this terrible time. He had a message for the parents of the young men caught up in this struggle. He asked them to turn in their children, as he called on the ruler to extend amnesty to all those who had taken up arms, even the killers of his own son. But no such peace was in the offing.

This mufti could not exonerate the regime or grant its deeds religious cover. In his hometown of Aleppo there had been a genuinely revered man of religion, the city's own mufti, Ibrahim al-Salqini. He had died of a brain hemorrhage in early September, and the rumors swirled that he had been done in by the regime. More likely, his had been a natural death at 77 years of age. But the mourners in his funeral procession had been certain that his death had come at the hands of the security forces. He was mourned as a "martyr," and his farewell ceremony had become a political demonstration of popular wrath against Bashar al-Assad. Salqini had been everything that Mufti Hassoun wasn't. He was learned and politically independent. He had stayed away from the regime, and he had offended the powers that be when he turned down an invitation, during the month of Ramadan, to attend an iftar (the breaking of the fast) with Bashar al-Assad. He had spoken against the "bloodbath" in the country and signed a petition, with other ulama in Aleppo, against the violence of the regime. He had warned that the quiet of Aleppo was deceptive and that the order was doomed unless it changed its ways. Syrians—and Aleppines in particular, in Mufti Hassoun's backyard —had a different model of what men of religion, *rijal al-din*, ought to do in the face of repressive rulers.

The grief over his son aside, Mufti Hassoun was back in the limelight a few days later. This time he was a regime functionary through and through. He had a message for Europe and America in a speech of fire and brimstone. At the first missile aimed at Syria and Lebanon, he said, "our sons and daughters will erupt and become 'suicidals' in your lands. Don't come close to our noble country." The young people of Syria and Lebanon will fight back, "an eye for an eye, a tooth for a tooth." He wanted this understood by America above all. On display was the talent—and more importantly, the political outlook—that raised Shaykh Hassoun to his exalted position. The Lebanese couldn't have missed the message. They were folded into Syria's world. Hafez al-Assad had long ago asserted that the Syrians and the Lebanese were "one people in two fraternal states"—a version of the Soviet view of its satellite regimes. Syria had since given a hesitant acceptance of Lebanese statehood, but the people of Lebanon were hostages in this Syrian crisis, and that was the message this cleric delivered.

The relationship between the Alawi-dominated regime and Sunni Islam was not straightforward. Mufti Hassoun wasn't of course the only member of the religious guild to make his accommodation with the rulers; many others did. For its part, the regime had paid tribute to Sunni Islam—the violation of mosques and the attacks on dissident ulama had come with the rebellion. Joshua Landis, one of the leading scholars of Syria in the American academy, put forward a proposition at odds with the image of a minoritarian regime warring against the dominant Sunni faith: "The Assads have struggled to be good Sunnis, not to make Sunnis into good liberals," he observed in a study of the educational curriculum in the country's schools: "Islamic education in Syrian schools is traditional, rigid, and Sunni. The Ministry of Education makes no attempt to inculcate notions of tolerance or respect for religious traditions other than Sunni Islam. Christianity is the one exception to this rule. Indeed, all religious groups other than Christians are seen to be enemies of Islam, who must be converted or fought against."

Landis examined the religious material assigned students in the fourth, fifth, seventh, ninth, and twelfth grades. Their content, he found, was pan-Arab and Sunni, the material was silent about the Alawis, the Ismailis, the Druze, and even about main-stream Shiism. The Alawi rulers had not wanted to awaken the furies of Sunni Islam. The "secularism" of the Baath was escape and evasion. Many of the "historic" leaders of the Baath hailed from the minorities—Greek Orthodox, Alawis, Druze, and Ismailis. No wonder the silence and deference to dominant Sunnism. A regime dispatching fierce jihadists into Iraq was bound to suffer a blowback. More importantly, that secular veneer would be torn by this tenacious rebellion. Landis writes that Syria had not chosen to follow a religious liberalism, but was such a path open to schismatics that ulama and laymen alike tolerated and grudgingly obeyed only because they had the means of repression and the big guns? Would a Sunni regime have fared better at "reform" of the religious tradition? On the face of it, it stands to reason that the answer to the second question would be in the affirmative. But after the 1980s and 1990s, and the fierce wind that blew over the Islamic world, one is best cautious in the face of the unknown and the untested.

As though to compensate for the menace of sectarianism, the opposition now insisted on its inclusiveness as some amulet against the menace. When a Syrian National Council was announced in Istanbul on October 2, its members were keen on displaying the diversity of this checkered society. The leadership of this council, as it was announced, would consist of five members from the Muslim Brotherhood and the tribes, four Kurds, a Christian, five "independents," six from the local coordination committees, and four from the "liberal current" led by an exiled academic based in Paris, Professor Burhan Ghalioun. There was even a seat for the small Assyrian community. In deference to the Kurds, the point was made that the next meeting would be held somewhere other than Turkey. The dispatches from Istanbul were silent about the matter of Alawi membership in the council. It is safe to assume that any such participation would have been given prominence had Alawis of stature been drawn into the opposition.

The sentiments in Istanbul were one thing, the outlines of a sectarian war on the ground altogether different. Syrians had of course been through this once before with the sectarian killings and the open warfare between the Muslim Brotherhood and the Alawis in the late 1970s and early 1980s. It had been a cruel and vicious time of targeted assassinations, the settling of scores, and the principal cities a theater for a running war across a sectarian divide. The political leaders of these new protests—old parliamentarians, journalists, activists drawn from the full spectrum of political life who had known prison and official cruelty—knew and feared that history. But the young rebels braving the tanks and the armored cars, risking life and limb, were free of the burden of that past. A discerning observer, the American journalist Anthony Shadid, who covered this story from Syria itself when he could and from Beirut, saw into that generational fault line. He dubbed the fearless breed of young men taking on the regime's forces: sons of no one. There was truth in that observation. The older generation had been beaten into submission, and the new generation was more daring. But the elders, it has been observed, had given a green light for this rebellion. This was their vicarious revolution, experienced through the heedlessness of their children.

CHAPTER EIGHT

Sarajevo on the Orontes

I F HAMA LENT ITS NAME—and trauma—to the events of the 1980s, this would be the era of Homs. This city had a high idea of itself as a pious and serious town and the burial place of Khalid bin al-Walid, the conqueror who had defeated the Byzantine Empire. It had supplied the country with three of its presidents and countless members of the political class— cabinet ministers, ambassadors, and more. It was in Homs and the towns in its orbit that the doubts about the efficacy of peaceful protest had crystallized. An expat from Homs, in a posting for *Syria Comment* on October 18, 2011, rightly dubbed Homs "the capital of the uprising." The writer, unnamed, provides a brief sketch of the city, its demography, and the changes that it underwent in recent years. It had been an overwhelmingly Sunni city, with a prosperous Christian minority that was approximately 10 percent of the population. An Ottoman census in 1903 listed a population of 51,000 people. (Homs now had 1.5 million inhabitants.) Like other towns in Greater Syria, Homs was led by notables, a cohesive group of merchant and religious families. A handful of these families owned most of the fertile land. The sweeping changes that remade Syria as a whole—the recruitment of the minorities into the armed forces, the rise of an ideologically driven younger generation through the Baath Party and the military—battered Homs and its old order. The notables were undermined, the city's demography altered. People from the countryside made their presence felt. The geography of the city responded to this influx, Christian newcomers occupied large parts of the Old City, and the Sunnis settled west, north, and east of the Old City walls. The Alawis were now a quarter of the population, huddled together in the southeastern quarter.

There was nothing unusual about this separation of the communities. All Ottoman cities were divided along confessional and religious lines. Homs turned inward in the late 1970s and early 1980s, as the defeat of its twin city, Hama, shook the self-confidence of the Sunnis of Homs as well. The Alawis were the regime's people and did not integrate well, this retrospect tells us. They were favored with government patronage, and they manned the *mukhabarat* and the security forces. Things were not idyllic in Homs, but the communities had managed a tolerable coexistence. An American diplomatic cable from 2010 drew on the testimonies of Melkite Catholic Archbishop Isidore Battikha and Greek Patriarchate Deputy Patriarch Father Afram. Their communities were thriving, the two religious leaders said. Their churches "enjoyed excellent relationships with their Muslim counterparts." Archbishop Battikha had served for fifteen years in Damascus prior to being transferred to the Homs diocese. It was better in Homs, he said, between the Muslims and the Christians, because the two populations lived "closer together." The archbishop was asked two or three times a year to speak in mosques, and it was his practice to invite imams to give speeches in his churches. The two groups did not pray together. Christianity was not endangered here. There were 45,000 Catholics in his diocese, second in size only to Damascus, and Father Afram said his Greek Orthodox church had stabilized at 150,000 after years of out-migration.

The peace of the city was punctured by this rebellion. This played out in a pattern familiar to those who followed the Lebanon war in the 1970s and 1980s and the ordeal of Sarajevo in the early 1990s. The neighborhoods of Homs split along sectarian fault lines—the Alawis and the Sunnis were at war with each other. (The Christians were not exactly equidistant between the two communities. They were allies of the Alawis and by and large committed to the regime.) The Sunnis had been moved not so much by Salafi extremism, we are told, but by the resentments over unequal access to economic opportunity and state patronage. On the face of it, this kind of proposition could be given credence. But the resentments were long in the making. The Sunnis from Homs had been waiting for deliverance—and retribution.

The town of Rastan, in Homs's orbit, had all but fallen to the rebellion by the closing days of August, and army defectors had made a stand there aided by the local population. A group of defectors went by a storied and meaningful name, the Khalid bin al-Walid Battalion. The name played on the de-legitimization of the Alawi regime as a reign of heretics and outsiders. Rastan lay on the main road to Aleppo, and Homs had grown increasingly defiant with its checkered neighborhoods at war with one another. The rebels had begun to target local figures of the regime and its known sympathizers. In response, the shabiha had gone on a rampage. The regime had to retrieve Rastan lest it emerge as a liberated city—and the base for a more determined insurgency. The regime's attack came in late September. Security forces backed by tanks and helicopters were dispatched to Rastan. The battle for the town had taken four days. The defectors had pulled out and their battalion had withdrawn to spare the town further killings, they announced. The security forces and the shabiha, the local vigilantes, commandeered hospitals and clinics and converted schools into detention centers. "Big losses," the regime's media routinely announced, were inflicted on the "armed terrorist groups."

The rebels had not prevailed, but the regime was nowhere close to being done with the upheaval. A tipping point may have been reached in Rastan and Homs, and the opposition was edging closer to turning into an armed insurrection. The conflict was becoming "weaponized," and arms were making their way into Homs and smuggled across Syria's porous borders. Elements of the regime were themselves selling weapons on the black market. Amid the violence, the people of Homs had grown braver still, taunting the dictator and prophesying his fall. It was as though Homs was taking pride in showing up Damascus and Aleppo and outdoing Hama. A measure of guilt played upon Syria's Sunni majority in that they had given in to the regime, that they had been cowed in the face of official terror, and that they had paid dearly for their old aversion to military service, the culture of guns, and martial ways. Now Homs was making up for all that, and the caution had been thrown overboard. The self-styled heirs of Khalid bin al-Walid were through with submission to a godless lot.

(Amid Homs's pain, a story broke in early October. Steve Jobs, the man who mastered our technological age, was the biological son of a man from Homs. Abdul Fattah "John" Jandali hailed from a Homs family of means. He had made his way to America in the early 1950s by way of the American University of Beirut. He had obtained a doctorate in political science from the University of Wisconsin. He had fathered a child out of wedlock and gave him up for adoption. This was the future Steve Jobs, who had grown up in the Bay Area. But in the manner of a people eager to see evidence of their success wherever it could be found, Jobs was now a "grandson of Homs." The Arabic electronic daily *Elaph* was flooded with Homsis and others straining for a connection to the wizard. "If you want another Steve Jobs, stop the killing of Syrian children," one posting to *Elaph* had it. Had Jobs been in Homs, an unsentimental posting read, he would have been protesting in the streets, or his father who would have been looking for him in the morgue or prison, as many parents in Homs had had to do.)

The regime was all in by now: its way was that of unrelenting violence. Bashar had no olive branches to offer. He had spoken three times to his country in the first phase of this conflict, and then he opted for silence. The protests were edging close to the capital. By October there were demonstrations near Bashar's presidential palace. The thinking of the man was conveyed through "guests" and interlocutors from Lebanon who had been summoned to Damascus for meetings with him. Two Sunni public figures, former Prime Ministers Salim al-Hoss from Beirut and Omar Karame from Tripoli, were put to cynical use. They came out of Bashar's bunker to say that the ruler was at ease with the condition of his country, that Syria had gone beyond the danger point and had put the events behind it, and that the "reforms" the president had in mind would see Syria to safe harbor. (Omar Karame was a man of little substance. Salim al-Hoss, in contrast, was a liberal figure of genuine standing, and his trip to Damascus was at variance with his record in public life.)

It was important for this embattled regime to convey a sense of mastery. A report went out that Bashar had told the Turkish foreign minister that he was capable of shattering the peace of the region in "no more than six hours." He would fire rockets across the Golan Heights into Israel, and he would call upon Hezbollah to launch its rockets into Tel Aviv. And further out, even the peace of the Persian Gulf would be shattered if Syria was cornered and subjected to a foreign invasion. Syria was not Libya, the ruler had said. (This was a variation on the theme of Syria's uniqueness, at the beginning of the Arab Spring, that Syria was not Tunisia or Egypt and was thus immune to popular upheaval.)

A break came the regime's way in early October courtesy of the United Nations Security Council. A toothless resolution had been brought to the Security Council containing a weak reference to the possibility of economic sanctions against Damascus. The resolution had the backing of the liberal democracies—the United States, Britain, and France. If the protesters in Syria needed illumination about the cruel ways of the world, the deliberations at the Security Council provided it. The resolution met with the double veto of Russia and China. The two big autocracies are invested in tyranny, and their vote was no surprise. On the narrowest of grounds, the Chinese had Tibet in mind and the Russians were thinking of the Chechens. Tyranny is indivisible, and popular protest is a menace to all these two autocracies embody and hold dear. (Russia has a naval base in the Syrian coastal city of Tartus, as the call of empire had not died out in Russia.)

In a note of supreme irony, Russia and China had used the conduct of NATO in Libya as a pretext for resisting any green light for the Western powers over the Syrian standoff. NATO, it is fair to say, had taken a Security Council resolution that author- ized the protection of Libyan civilians and ran with it. The pro- tection of Libyan civilians had turned into a warrant for unseating the Qaddafi regime. China and Russia would draw a line when it came to Syria.

The sordid vote at the Security Council over Syria was an indictment of the three "emerging" powers that abstained on so simple a proposition—India, Brazil, and South Africa. If these powers were making a bid for a more prominent role in the world, if their conduct was a bid for a permanent role on the Security Council, their moral abdication was proof that they were not ready to shoulder the burden of maintaining a decent international order. The shame of India, the world's largest democracy, was all its own. India is forever thinking of Kashmir, and the principle of unfettered national sovereignty must be maintained at all cost. There was not much to say about Brazil and South Africa. Their exalted view of themselves is preening and illusion. Brazil was said to have bought the Syrian regime's claim that its survival was a shield for the Christians. South Africa came into this affair with a dishonorable performance in the Libyan saga behind it. The tyranny of Muammar el-Qaddafi never troubled Pretoria, and the "king of kings of Africa" had squandered plenty of his people's treasure buying off the consent and approval of so many African states.

Judging by its conduct in the immediate aftermath of the Security Council resolution, the regime took that vote as a green light for a heavier dosage of repression still. On October 7 a noted Kurdish leader in the opposition, Mashaal Tammo, was assassinated in his hometown of Qamishli in the northeast. Tammo, who headed a small Kurdish party, had served a three-year prison sentence for his activism. In the spectrum of Kurdish sentiments, Tammo was an assimilationist. His party sought the integration of the Kurds into mainstream national political life. He was a member of the newly formed Syrian National Council. The Kurds, no less than 10 percent of the Syrian population, had been wary of the protests. They had worried about the national chauvinism of the Arabs, and they were not happy with the influence that Turkey had come to exercise over the Syrian rebellion.

Qamishli, the principal Kurdish city in the country, had known sporadic protests, and all had been small in size. Now with this crime, the regime had pushed the Kurds into the opposition. A crowd of no fewer than 50,000 people poured into the streets of Qamishli—in defiance of the government. The security forces fired into the funeral procession, and two mourners were killed. The regime was busy making its own enemies. True to form, the official media said a black car with four armed men fired at Tammo, killing him and wounding his son.

Goons and bullies do what they do. The regime had given its vigilantes a license to frighten off noted figures of the opposition. The political cartoonist Ali Ferzat, arguably the most famous and accomplished in his craft in the Arab world, was given a savage beating. His hands were broken, and he was left bleeding by the side of the road on the way to the Damascus airport. Before the attack on him, his most recent cartoon depicted Qaddafi in his jeep picking up Bashar al-Assad, who was hitching a ride. In Homs, the aged parents of a distinguished pianist, Malek Jandali, were assaulted in their home. Their son had taken part in an anti-regime event in the United States, and the parents, an old physician and an equally accomplished spouse, were to be punished for the sins of their son. Riad Seif, a former parliamentarian and an activist who had done his own stint in the regime's prisons, was beaten in broad daylight as he left a centrally located mosque in the heart of Damascus. Riad Seif was not in the best of health. He had been battling cancer, and this humiliation and violence by the security forces was not going to deter him. His membership in the Syrian National Council was public, and because he was inside the country while so many oppositionists were abroad, he was within reach. Yet another critic of the regime, former parliamentarian Mamoun al-Homsi, was punished; his son was picked up and taken away by the security forces. The Syrian rulers were now out to show that they were beyond censure or limits.

This display of open contempt for the exhortations and condemnations leveled at the regime masked a nervousness on the part of the rulers. For all this petty bravado, Syria was not Russia or China; it was not even Iran, its regional ally and protector. Bashar and the ruling cabal around him lacked the wealth and the weight needed to sustain a tyranny that runs afoul of the norms of decent conduct. There was no wealth to cushion the dictatorship; oil exports provided the regime with a third of its income, and now these exports were subjected to effective sanctions. Bashar, like his father before him, had secured the support of the business classes and the merchants in Damascus and Aleppo with a political economy of favoritism and bureaucratic preferences—crony capitalism in its purest form. Now the beneficiaries of this regime had begun to worry whether the edifice will stand. There were reports that the monied classes—big Sunni and Christian interests—had begun to hedge their bet and invest in the rebellion. The confidence of the ruling cabal had cracked. On September 22, a decision was made to suspend imports of goods that have over 5 percent customs duties—effectively most of the country's imports that matter. The economy was brought to a standstill, and the business class that had averted its gaze from the repression came out in full against this ban. Twelve days later, the government gave in. Gone was the bravado that the ban on imports would help Syria overcome the sanctions imposed by the United States and the European Union. Thus the pressure was on to be done with the rebellion, to subdue the population before economic collapse set in. Even the dreaded shabiha, the regime's vigilantes doing its killings and barbarisms, had to be paid. Their excesses mounted as they were unleashed on ordinary Syrians to extort from them what the regime itself could no longer provide.

The bluff of the Syrian rulers was being called; Russia had given cover to the regime at the United Nations Security Council, but days later, the Russian President Dmitri Medvedev let it be known that there were limits to Russia's indulgence. Syria was in need of reforms, Medvedev observed, and "if the Syrian leadership is incapable of conducting such reforms, it will have to go. But this decision would be taken not in NATO or certain European countries. It should be taken by the Syrian people and the Syrian leadership."

THIS REGIME had risen out of the military. It had enlisted security and paramilitary forces from outside the army. For decades, the nation's army had been honored and praised. It stood to reason that the protesters would hope that the army would break ranks and that defections would seal its fate. In that spirit Friday, October 14, was named the Friday of the Free Army—seven full months after the eruption of the rebellion. The killing machine was relentless, and 21 people were struck down on that day. To be sure, there had been defections. Bands of soldiers and their officers, doubtless Sunnis, had broken ranks. There were videos of them flashing their army identity cards and speaking in earnest of the reasons for their defection. There had been clashes between the defectors and the regime's forces. But the mutiny hoped for by the protesters had not materialized. The Assad regime may not have mastered the skills of developing a decent, prosperous society. But it had to be granted the men of the regime that they knew how to put together a formidable system of repression. They could rely of course on the loyalty of the Alawis, but it wasn't just sectarian loyalty that held the regime together. There was ruthlessness aplenty and skill in the way the military units were deployed.

A sense of this system in place was given Agence France-Presse by defectors who had made their way to Lebanon. It was kill or be killed in the ranks of the army. A 25-year-old lieutenant from the central province of Homs supplied details of the workings of the army. Four months earlier, he had been off duty, in his village, when the army raided the place. He could not bear what he had witnessed. Soldiers had burst into the home of a suspected activist. They had shot the man's wife and daughters in the legs to force them to reveal the man's whereabouts. A 20-year-old soldier, also from Homs, said his unit was often told to shoot at innocent bystanders. "I saw with my own eyes an unarmed older farmer in a village in Homs province go by on a bicycle, and we were ordered to shoot him in the back." An efficient political army had been put together—Sunni recruits, Alawi commanders, and battalions from different brigades thrown together. These soldiers didn't know each other and had no history of familiarity and comradeship. The soldiers were never in doubt that they themselves would be struck down if they didn't follow their orders. From the young lieutenant again: "I got out because I need to live with a clear conscience. I joined the army to protect my people and my land, to free the Golan, not Homs and Deraa."

The military units were given orders to "kill or kill"—kill the protesters or kill those soldiers who refuse to obey orders. Soldiers were banned from using cell phones, they could watch only state television, and they were given a steady diet of lectures about the goodness of the Assad family and the benevolence of the leader. The soldiers were deployed up front, the mukhabarat operatives behind them. Snipers on rooftops would fire at soldiers pointed out to them by the officers and the mukhabarat. Soldiers who wanted out of the killing and stopped firing could be summarily executed on the spot. The military uniform offered no protection. The regime and its intelligence agencies had prepared for this moment.

Ahmad, from Aleppo, posted a short message on Al Jazeera on October 20, on learning of the killing of Qaddafi: *Mabrook* (congratulations), he said to the people of Libya, may the same thing happen here in Syria. That case of "Libya envy" was on display, Libyans had gotten rid of their tyrant, and the Syrians were still in the thick of their fight, the eighth month of their war against the regime had just opened. The rulers were still insisting on the "specialness" of Syria, on its immunity to the fate that had befallen the reigns of Zine el-Abidine Ben Ali in Tunisia, Mubarak in Egypt, and Qaddafi in Libya. Abandoned by their armed forces, the Tunisian and Egyptian strongmen had packed it in. Bashar and the ruling cabal had no intention of giving in. The crack units defending the regime were invested in it, and their very safety derived from the regime's survival. As for the Libyan case, the Syrian rulers were confident that it held no relevance for them. Indeed, in a note of cruel irony, the deliverance of Libya was used by the Russians and the Chinese as a case of a NATO operation that overreached, that took a yellow light at the United Nations Security Council as a warrant for overthrowing the Libyan dictator. For the Russians and the Chinese, there would be no more interventions of the Libyan variety. For its part, the Syrian regime told its own people, and Arabs beyond, that its place in the Arab constellation of power dwarfed that of the erratic Libyan ruler. Syria took pride in being a founding member of the Arab League, with her rights and prerogatives in that body way beyond those claimed by Qaddafi.

There was no likelihood that the Arab League, which had authorized a NATO operation in the name of defending the civilian population of Libya, would do the same in the Syrian case. And truth be known, the Arab League had not proven the Damascus regime wrong. In October, Syria was given a reprieve of fifteen days for the regime to bring an end to the violence against the protests. The rebellion had always been rich in iconography, with poignant messages on placards held up to the cameras. One such placard from Homs now noted that the Syrian people were being massacred "with the permission of the Arab League." Nabil El-Araby, the secretary-general of the Arab League and an honest international jurist, conceded the weakness of his organization. He had no forces at his disposal. Only the United Nations Security Council had the power to compel member states to alter their ways. Stoicism had settled upon the protesters. One telling proclamation held up to the camera simply read, "With us is God," *Maana Allah*. The fight between the irresistible force and the immovable object had not been settled. Bashar and the "killing machine" around him were doing their best to break the will of the population, to tell them that they are alone in the world and that the state possessed formidable means of repression at home and diplomatic assets abroad. There were oppositionists who fled the regime's wrath to Lebanon, and they were particularly vulnerable. They had crossed the border into a Syrian protectorate, and the regime could reach into Lebanon directly, kidnap its opponents, liquidate them at will, and have its way through its pliable Lebanese surrogates. There were friends of Syria's liberty in Lebanon, public figures and intellectuals, who understood the linkage between Syria's liberty and their own. But the Syrian eruption had happened when a Hezbollah-led government in Beirut was allied with the Damascus regime. "There is no safety in Lebanon," a man from the border town of Tell Kalakh said from his refuge in Wadi Khaled, in Lebanon's northernmost corner, a valley that juts into Syria. "The government in Lebanon is allied to the Syrian regime, and that is not a secret."

The servile cabinet of Prime Minister Najib Mikati promised protection for the Syrian refugees—there were about 3,000 of them—but no credence would be given that promise. The Lebanese rulers had not protected their own against Syrian cruelty, and they would not risk the wrath of Damascus on behalf of Syrians fleeing the fire. No Syrian opponent of the regime was safe in Lebanon. The terror took in the prominent and the humble alike. A laborer distributing leaflets against the regime was picked up, along with two of his brothers, and the three of them were spirited off to Syria. The authorities in Beirut suspected that a Lebanese security officer had been an accomplice in the kidnapping. And there was a more noted case of abduction. In late May, 89-year-old Shibli al-Aismay, one of the early leaders of the Baath who had lost out in the party's fratricidal wars, went out for his daily walk in a once-tranquil town in Mount Lebanon and never returned. Aismay had come to Lebanon from the United States, where he had been living, to visit his daughter and perhaps to oversee the publication of his memoirs. The man, a Druze, had had no political role since 1966, when Michel Aflaq and the "founding fathers" of the party were overthrown by a younger generation of officers. But the regime had taken no chances, and Lebanese security officers uncovered the evidence of a kidnapping tied to the Syrian Embassy in Beirut.

Courage had not deserted the Lebanese. Nayla Tueni, the publisher of *An-Nahar* and now a bearer of her father's torch, wrote a scathing column on October 31 titled, "Don't Turn Lebanon into a Syrian Prison." "Lebanon was once a refuge for all the oppressed in the Arab world, particularly for those who sought freedom of opinion and belonging. It is being turned into a prison and an instrument of Syrian repression, a regime that practiced all sorts of tyranny and torture against the Lebanese before it turned its wrath against its own people."

The terms of engagement in Syria had not altered; it was a race for time between the regime and the protesters. The rulers knew the economics of their tyranny. They were running down their financial reserves. The sanctions imposed on the sale of oil had worked, and the patience of the merchant class in Aleppo and Damascus and the indulgence they had granted the regime had their limits. On the other side, the multitudes risking all in their attempt to topple the regime were up against the limits of endurance. People can't indefinitely live on their nerves, go out day after day, and face heavily armed forces of order and vigilantes. Privation is always a factor in these great contests of will—the shortages of food and medicine, and the burden of securing daily necessities. The rhythm of normal life had been shattered. Schooling for the young had been interrupted. "Today a school, tomorrow a detention center," the placard of one schoolboy read during this time. There was no meaning for schooling without liberty, defiant schoolchildren proclaimed. The regime wasn't stepping aside, and the protesters were not calling off their rebellion.

A YOUNG BOY of 15 or 16 in stylish sunglasses holds up a sign reading, "If I weren't Syrian I would want to be Libyan." This was late October, and this boy and others taking to the streets had witnessed the killing of the Libyan dictator. This had given them heart. They could see in the punishment of Qaddafi a prelude of what they wanted for their own dictator. Authority was being stripped of its magic: Saddam Hussein had been flushed out of his spider hole in 2003, Hosni Mubarak had been turning up at court on a gurney, and now Qaddafi had been dragged out of a drainage pipe. Friday, October 28, was named the Friday for the No-Fly Zone. The reticence about foreign help was giving way, and pride was yielding to necessity. Samir Nashar, a noted member of the umbrella opposition group, the Syrian National Council, gave a forthright assessment of the standoff with the regime. Foreign intervention and civil war were terrible options, he said, and most Syrians rejected these alternatives, but the worst possible outcome was the survival of the regime. "That last possibility had no definite shelf life for Bashar inherited power from his father and could yet bequeath it to his son. We don't live in the colonial age. Here before us is the Libyan precedent. Had it not been for military intervention, Qaddafi would have exterminated the people of Benghazi."

The cruelty of the regime was making a mockery of the "red lines" of the opposition and the pieties of nationalism. Homs was now a city under siege, short of bread, water, and provisions. Shops whose owners supported the regime were selling things at a premium, and those whose owners supported the protests had been subjected to theft or arson. That Friday was particularly grim: the cities of Homs and Hama had been targeted, 40 people were killed, and hundreds were rounded up. This was the bloodiest day in over five months. Vigilantes on motorbikes were randomly shooting people in Homs. An old district of the city—a

Sunni neighborhood—was shelled. The regime understood the import of this day. Sure enough, no NATO planes were on the runways on their way toward Syria, but the rulers couldn't be fully certain that the outside world could withstand indefinite carnage in Syria. A hawkish United States senator, John McCain, who had played no small part in the debate over Libya, had begun to make the case for intervention in Syria. A regime given to a healthy dosage of paranoia could not be certain about the play in the Western democracies. Sure enough, the regime in Damascus had taken the measure of the Arab League. On October 16, the Arab League in a Cairo meeting had ruled out foreign intervention and trade sanctions, and had even refused to suspend Syria's membership in the League. But NATO and the Turkish state next door could not be taken for granted.

The change in Turkey's attitude was a source of worry. The Turks were now giving shelter and asylum to Syrian army defectors. A no-fly zone and a protected area on the border that could serve as a magnet for army defectors and insurgents had to be duly considered. The script had not varied. The regime's assaults were the policy of rulers in a hurry to prevail. Time and again, the protests and their size and intensity confounded the regime's expectations that it had ridden out the worst of it. For its part, the regime had long obliterated the "red lines" that rulers observe if the most rudimentary form of social contract is to be maintained. Mosques had long ceased to be inviolable and off-limits, and violence was now visited on hospitals and clinics. Amnesty International, in a report issued on October 25, documented a pattern of systematic abuse and cruelty. Security forces had been given the run of hospitals, and the medical staff were taking part in the torture and ill treatment of their patients. National hospitals in Baniyas, Homs, and Tell Kalakh had been particularly egregious. As blood supplies could be obtained only from the

Central Blood Bank—controlled by the Ministry of Defense—
doctors were faced with a terrible dilemma. The requests for
blood entailed putting the patients at risk of arrest, torture, or
possibly death in custody. There is a social capital born of modernity and often acquired in the face of difficult odds, and this
health care system was part of it—physicians, nurses, and other
caregivers brought up to some decent professional norms. Now
this heritage was of the past, the regime destroying this last vestige of a secure public order. Patients were awakening from trau-
mas to nurses in white robes armed with clubs and rifles. Hospital
workers and physicians suspected of sympathizing with the
wounded were savagely beaten by the security forces.

The opposition was not chastened, but its leaders conceded
that the regime had the advantage in the weekend that followed
the Friday for the No-Fly Zone. At least 60 people were reported
killed, and Homs had come in for another dose of violence. No
deliverance was within sight, and Bashar al-Assad put on a brave
face. He fell back yet again on the standing of Syria in a sensitive
and volatile region in an interview he gave to *The Sunday Telegraph* on October 30: "Syria is the hub now in this region. It is
the fault line and if you play with the ground you will cause an
earthquake—do you want to see another Afghanistan, or tens of
Afghanistans? Any problem in Syria will burn the whole region."
His regime, he said, made some early mistakes. It had not been
ready for the eruption, but things had improved and the security
forces now targeted only terrorists. Diplomacy was moribund, the
(mild) threats of the Arab League were hollow, and a mediation
effort sponsored by the League had called upon "both sides" to
stop the violence, which could only have fortified Assad's will.
The Qatari Foreign Minister Hamad bin Jassem al-Thani, who
had played a pivotal role in the struggle that overthrew the

Qaddafi regime, warned that the entire region was "at risk of a massive storm." The League urged Syria to withdraw its tanks from the streets, but this was to no avail.

The regime's assets were not yet spent. There was the Free Syrian Army of the defectors, but they were no match for the security forces. Their leader, a colonel, spoke from Turkey. He appeared, it was learned, in a suit given him by his Turkish handlers. Turkey had effectively turned on Bashar, but it had not set out to topple him. NATO representatives and leaders were running a victory lap for their performance over Libya—they had declared the completed mission a brilliant success—but the gift given Libya was not there for the Syrians. Arab pilots and aircraft from Qatar, the United Arab Emirates, and Jordan had taken part in the Libyan campaign. Qatar had been particularly assertive and had even sent special forces to Libya. But the Syrian oppositionists were on their own.

Washington had not taken up the cause of this rebellion. President Obama, the standard-bearer of American power, had gone half-in into the Libyan endeavor. Syria was a bridge too far. President Obama had his eye on his bid for a second term. He would be taking into that bid the proud claim that he fulfilled a promise by ending the war in Iraq; he would not saddle himself with another conflict in the Fertile Crescent. There had been these early hopes invested in Bashar, which the diplomatic cables from Damascus had confirmed. Early on, there was the cautious reading of the balance of forces between the regime and the opposition. The American position would undergo a slow, painful change, which was no great comfort to the rebellion. On April 22, the White House had called on Assad to "change course now and heed the calls of his own people." "Meaningful reforms" were overdue, but the rulers had "placed their personal interests ahead of the Syrian people." On July 11 came a stronger statement, this time from the secretary of state: "President Assad is not indispensible, and we have absolutely nothing invested in him remaining in power. If anyone, including President Assad, thinks that the United States is secretly hoping that the regime will emerge from this turmoil to continue its brutality and repression, they are wrong." On August 12, the secretary of state gave away the ambivalence in American policy. By now, the repression was five months and counting: "There are Syrian opposition figures outside of Syria and inside. But there's no address for the opposition. There is no place any of us who wish to assist can go." There were "multiple return addresses" by then—in Deraa, Hama, Baniyas, and Jisr al-Shughour—but the American statements were an honest reflection of an unwillingness to take the lead on Syrian matters. It would be in a statement, on August 18, that President Obama would finally call on the Syrian ruler to step aside. "We have consistently said that President Assad must lead a democratic transition or get out of the way. He has not led. For the sake of the Syrian people, the time has come for President Assad to step aside."

The reluctance to make that call on Assad to leave office was understandable. The critics clamor for such a call, and they were doing so in this Syrian case. This statement made and the noncoercive options spent, it is now either anticlimactic or a resort to arms. President Obama had been clear in every way that there was no interest in unseating the Assad regime by force of arms. In a perfect world, these Syrian protesters would be given the rarest of gifts. The Americans would unseat this despot—and then locate him somewhere in a spider hole or a drainage pipe—without the Syrian oppositionists openly asking for military help. But the world, we know, does not grant such wishes.

For well over four months, Bashar al-Assad had stayed out of the limelight, the foreign media effectively kept out of Syria. But by late October, he and his handlers made themselves available. It wasn't exactly free-for-all media access, but the regime was keen to display its serenity and tell its side of the story. This slight opening was perhaps to convey the message that the regime had prevailed and now had nothing to hide. In a rapid succession, Bashar gave an interview to Russia's Channel One and two interviews to *The Sunday Telegraph*. Bouthaina Shaaban, one of his trusted aides and a literature professor, made herself available to *The Independent*. A reporter for *The Washington Post* was allowed into Damascus accompanied by security officers. British reporter Andrew Gilligan, who interviewed the ruler for *The Sunday Telegraph*, was permitted access to Hama.

The modernizer who spent two years in London turned up for the interviews. Andrew Gilligan was met in a modest bungalow by the ruler dressed in jeans. He was Dr. Bashar again, the policy wonk. The protests were fading, he said, their roots were not mainly political: "It's about the whole of society, the development of society. Different problems have erupted as one crisis. We adopted liberal economics. To open your economy without preparing yourself, you open up gaps between the social strata. If you do not get the right economic model, you can't get past the problem." There was his heralded leadership of the Syria Computer Society, and that computer literacy was on display as well. Comparing Syria's leadership with that of a Western country was akin to comparing a Mac to a PC. "Both computers do the same job, but they don't understand each other. You need to translate. If you want to analyze me as the East, you cannot analyze me through the Western operating system. You have to translate according to my operating system or culture." Told by the reporter that this was the "inner nerd" in him speaking, he laughed out loud, and the reporter was pleased that he had gotten away with the banter. The ruler was a popular man, he said of himself: "I live a normal life, we have neighbors, I take my kids to school, that's why I am popular. It is very important to live this way—that is the Syrian style."

Two days later, the same reporter was in Hama, trailed by "minders" of course. He found a "city of fear and ghosts." There were snipers in the old Byzantine citadel positioned to fire at will into the streets, and the people the reporter encountered were on edge. They were in no mood for revelations. The governor said the city was at peace—at least 90 percent so. "The key thing we did was spreading the culture of love and cooperation with the people." Inside the governor's office there were screens showing closed-circuit TV pictures from around the city, "just in case any further lack of love or cooperation should occur," the reporter added.

It was like this in Bashar al-Assad's realm: the alternation of light and darkness, the regime's Janus-like face to be shown the outside world and the fearsome crackdown. It was in that vein on November 3 that the regime would announce its acceptance of an Arab League initiative to end the fighting as 34 people were struck down by the violence. In Homs, a placard summed up the judgment of the protesters: "The Arab League and the Syrian regime, two sides of the same coin." The rupture between the regime and the populace was given away by a deed that must have drawn inspiration from Libya, where the people discarded the green flag of Qaddafi for the flag of the monarchy: Syria's old flag of independence was unfurled for the first time in the outskirts of Damascus. The country was seeking its second independence— and this time from the tyranny within.

CHAPTER NINE

The Stalemate

FOR ALL THE heavy odds they faced, the opponents of the regime were trying to put forth the semblance of an alternative. On November 6, the eve of Eid al-Adha, the feast of sacrifice, the head of the Syrian National Council, Professor Burhan Ghalioun, secured airtime on Al Jazeera for a statement to the "great Syrian people." Flanked by a bookshelf on one side and a Syrian flag on the other, Burhan Ghalioun had the air of a national leader in the making, the embodiment of the non-Bashar way, if you will. Syria will no longer be anyone's farm, Ghalioun said, but a state of rights and laws. "Your courage had stirred the admiration of the world. With each passing day and every drop of blood shed, we are one step closer to freedom." He spoke of the Kurds, who will receive the rights they were long denied. In the new Syrian polity there will be no talk of majority and minorities, and the country that the regime had turned into a "big prison" will become the homeland of all. He thanked the soldiers who refused to obey unjust orders and warned those who were trampling on the rights of the population that they will not be able to acquit themselves on grounds that they were merely following orders. He spoke to those on the fence, who are "afraid or hesitant," and told them that this was their revolution and that this newly formed national council was theirs and a way of getting their voice heard.

The speech was free of bluster, and the man delivering it was a
French-educated political sociologist. His books had always been
abstract, at times impenetrable, with a leftist bent. Doubtless, he
was aware that he was speaking from the safety of his base of
exile in Paris, in an ordered land, and a long absence from Syria.
Ghalioun was born in Homs in 1945, and he had left in 1970 as
the country was slipping under the control of Hafez al-Assad. He
recalled his youth as a time when Syria was whole. His father was
a horse breeder, and the son would ride "across open vistas to the
east of Homs, landscapes that have disappeared today." In the
ways of exiles savoring places adorned and prettified by memory,
he recalls jumping on stones to cross the Orontes River. He loved
the *maqam* (the shrine) of the Caliph Umar bin Abdulaziz, a
"simple structure on a small hill" where he would read his books
in the shade. He savored the memory of the Ghouta, the gardens
and orchards on the outskirts of Damascus, places at once "spec-
tacular and soothing." For matters political, he was a young
devotee of the Egyptian leader Gamal Abdel Nasser, and now a
half-century later, he still believes that the breakup of the short
union between Syria and Egypt was a mistake. There was political
tumult all around then and not all of it was coherent and thought-
out, but all that was snuffed out, he says, when Assad came to
power, "rule turned Fascist," and it was "the end of political life
in Syria."

That Homs of yesteryear was politically and physically gone,
and the city of Ghalioun's birth was now the theater for a terrible
war. There had been talk of the Arab initiative to bring the violence to an end, but over the space of five days, the local coordination committees that organize and document the protests
estimated that 111 people in Homs had been killed. There was a
grim report that a microbus had been attacked and eleven Alawis

in it had been killed. Baba Amr, a Sunni neighborhood, was being shelled daily. Homsis were beyond the claims of nationalism, the Alawi neighborhoods were now enemy territory, and the Christians trying to wait out the violence were accomplices of the regime.

The rulers were keen to erase the line between combatants and ordinary people caught up in this struggle. The Alawi community was being pressed into the fight. Protesters from the Sunni town of Tell Kalakh were bused to a nearby Alawi village. One protester recalled the incident. The villagers were told to come out "and beat these traitors, and if any of them pigs dies, just throw them away. The villagers then started beating us with fists and feet and shovel handles, saying, 'you want freedom, here is your freedom.' "

There was one consoling episode, the kind that Homsis and others in Syria pointed to as evidence of their country's unity and secularism. Prominent actress Fadwa Soliman, an Alawite born in Aleppo who was active in the protests over the preceding eight months, turned up in Homs in support of the embattled city. She was Syrian, she proclaimed, and this regime was not hers. The regime had deceived the minorities, she said. She had no apologies to offer, and days later, members of her family would disown her. On national television, they said she was a traitor tempted by fame and fortune. The regime had claimed its own community, and it was hazardous for an Alawite to cross the line. Fadwa Soliman went into hiding, as the vigilantes were looking for her.

Much to the surprise of the Syrian rulers, the patience and indulgence of the Arab League was not unlimited. On November 16, the League finally suspended Syria's membership in that organization. The consensus was nearly universal. Only Yemen and Lebanon stood by the Damascus regime, and Iraq abstained. The

eighteen other members of the League had had their fill of the
Syrian rulers. They were listening to "the street" in their own
lands. The brutality—and the brazenness—had stirred the most
reluctant of states to break with Damascus. Was this a case of
Sunni sympathy for the rebellion? If so, that must have played a
minor role, I believe. There was a straightforward explanation: a
genuine sense of outrage at the cruelty. This struggle in Syria was
playing out against a big Arab disturbance. The Egyptian and
Tunisian rulers had called it quits, and the Libyan had received
his comeuppance. Bashar had held on and seemed to defy the
odds—and the very laws of gravity. The expectations of another
domino falling, another dictator swept out of power by popular
upheaval, had not been fulfilled. The custodians of power in the
Arab capitals and at the headquarters of the Arab League had
taken their cue from public sentiment. No ruler was quite as egregious as Qaddafi, as odd and "undomesticated," but Bashar
al-Assad had made his own way out of the club of acceptable
rulers. He now had the Iraqi firebrand Muqtada al-Sadr, and
Hezbollah in Beirut, as companions of the road. The rulers in the
saddle had drawn their own conclusions: the man in Damascus
was not likely to find his way back into their ranks.

In what had become standard fashion, the protesters gave
Friday, November 25, a name: The Free Army Protects Me. The
army defectors had begun to make their presence felt, and the
sense that the rebellion would have to win its own war was more
widespread now. An ambush on the Palmyra-Homs road set up
by the Free Army had just killed six elite pilots and four support
staff. The balance of raw power had not been radically trans-
formed, but the defectors had begun to give heart to the rebellion.
The Arab governments had given the regime yet another extension before they imposed their own economic sanctions, and

Damascus had stalled. It had no interest in allowing Arab monitors into the country, and it insisted that the sanctions held out
by the Arab governments were an empty threat. Arab diplomacy
invoked the threat of "internationalizing" the matter of the
regime's brutality. But here, too, the Syrian rulers had the Russians and the Chinese to bail them out at the United Nations
Security Council. A French proposal had surfaced: the setting up
of "humanitarian corridors" through which food and medicine
would be made available to the civilian centers that needed it.
Without fail the Russians had dismissed this idea and said the
only way out of this crisis was through internal Syrian dialogue.
Deep down, those who had risen against the regime had understood the terms of this contest: it was either the tyranny of the
Assads or the terrible price of a rebellion.

On November 27, the Arab League raised the stakes with the
last arrow in its quiver: it approved economic sanctions against
Damascus. The measures included a travel ban against nineteen
of the regime's most powerful figures (including a half-dozen
members of the Assad family), a halt to transactions with the
Syrian Central Bank, and an end to Arab economic projects in
Syria. All three Arab countries that border Syria—Lebanon,
Jordan, and Iraq—were dubious of these new measures. Lebanon
"disassociated" itself from the vote, Jordan had given its approval
but expressed unease over the sanctions, and Iraq abstained. Lebanon was a Syrian protectorate and was forgiven its timidity.
Jordan's trade was hugely dependent on the Syrian ports of Tartus
and Latakia; 40 percent of Jordan's imports came through these
two port cities. There was a large Iraqi community of refugees in
Syria, and the authorities in Baghdad said their interests would
be harmed by these punitive measures. (In a supreme note of
irony, Iraqi President Jalal Talabani, who was the beneficiary of

an American war that upended the Saddam regime and brought
him to the apex of power, opined that he opposed armed Western
intervention in the internal affairs of the states of the region. He
did not question the rights of the Syrian people to democracy and
liberties, he said, but he was against any Turkish or Western military intervention in Syria.)

The Syrian rulers described the Arab sanctions as an "economic war" on Syria as they belittled the very same measures.
The Syrian pound had lost 25 percent of its value since the onset
of the rebellion, but the regime put on a brave face. Their country
was self-sufficient, they insisted. It would feed itself and was
immune to outside pressure. By the close of November, the
regime had found an odd release: it had become a rogue state,
embattled and isolated. It had broken with the Arab world—and
this was the Baathist regime that trumpeted Syria's specialness as
the "beating heart of Arabism." There were reports that the tiny
emirate of Qatar, which had played an outsize role in the demoli-
tion of the Qaddafi regime, was determined to spare no funds to
be rid of the Assad regime. It was rumored that the Qataris had
pledged that they would bankroll a Turkish assault against the
Syrian rulers. And to further dramatize Syria's isolation, the
United Nations Human Rights Council would weigh in with a
detailed report charging the regime with "crimes against human-
ity." The Syrian government had not cooperated, the international investigators had done their best, and some 220 victims
and/or witnesses, including army defectors, had come forth with
evidence of rampant lawlessness. The "legalese" of the document
served only to highlight the brutality of the regime's doings. The
protesters had all the knowledge they needed as to the misdeeds
of the security forces, but they now had the authority of a world
body with moral standing. Soldiers had been given liberty to kill

at random, hospitals had become places of torture and killings, and arbitrary arrests had taken place in Homs, Hama, Deraa, Baniyas, and elsewhere. Soldiers suspected of sympathizing with the protesters were detained, many of them subjected to torture. Children were also tortured, some to death, the report confirmed. An army defector who aimed high at a crowd to avoid causing injury was caught and accused of being a "secret agent." He was beaten and tortured with electroshock. Sexual torture and humiliation were part of the security forces' arsenal. A 2-year-old girl in Latakia was shot and killed by an officer who said he did not want her to grow up and become a demonstrator. The regime was done with the pretense of being one with the order of nations. No one was quite certain of the death toll. The United Nations' high commissioner for human rights announced that a threshold had been crossed. By November's end the estimates of those killed had reached 4,000 and could go much higher.

November turned out to be the cruelest of months in which 950 people were killed. It would be fair to say that the expectations of the regime and those who had risen to challenge it had not been fulfilled. The rebellion was not crushed, and the regime had not fallen. Outsiders mattered but thus far not decisively. Iran was doing all it could to bail out the rulers, and the Arab world and Turkey were giving heart to the rebellion. The pan-Arab media—principally the television channels Al Jazeera and Al Arabiya—had made the Syrian upheaval their dominant focus.

This struggle *in* Syria was also a struggle *for* Syria. A high-stakes regional contest was playing out, with Syria as the prize and the background. On one side were arrayed Turkey, Saudi Arabia, and the smaller states of the Gulf, with the United States and France in the background; on the other side were the Damascus regime, its Hezbollah ally in Beirut, a "soft" partnership with

Baghdad, and Iran as the leader of this group. (It could be said that Russia and China were in the remote background as backers of Syria, but these two autocracies were cheating and Syria was not such a priority for them.) In one of the clichés of the time of Old Man Assad, it was proudly, and rightfully, claimed for the man that he changed Syria from a plaything to a player in the region. The reference was to the late 1940s and 1950s when Syria was weak in the scales of power and was being fought over by Egypt, Iraq, and Saudi Arabia. Once again, under Bashar, Syria was an object of a wider contest. Syria had provided Iran with access to the Mediterranean and gave the Persian state a role in Arab affairs. The Syrian-Iranian relationship had been forged by Hafez al-Assad in the early 1980s. But as the historian Itamar Rabinovich rightly notes, the relationship had changed under Bashar and become one of subservience to Iran. The freedom to maneuver enjoyed by the father had been lost. Damascus was now a satrap of the Iranian theocracy.

The protagonists in this struggle fully understood that a Syria ruled by a Sunni majority would turn away from Iran and Hezbollah. There was sectarianism at play. The Sunni pact of states would be strengthened, and the Iran-led axis would be dealt a serious blow. The Palestinian movement Hamas, a die-hard Sunni movement, was in the crossfire. Its functionaries made their adjustment in a move dubbed "soft exit." They quietly reduced their presence in Damascus as the regime's prospects darkened, and then they left Damascus for Gaza and Cairo. Hamas did not want to be cut off from the wider Arab world. By the raw calculations of power, a radical alliance was pitted against status quo powers. Burhan Ghalioun, the leader of the Syrian National Council, foresaw a change in Syria's place in the affairs of the region. "There will be no special relationship with Iran.

Breaking the exceptional relationship means breaking the strategic, military alliance." This alliance with Iran had drifted into a relationship of subservience on the part of the Bashar al-Assad regime, and the rebellion in Deraa, Homs, and Hama wanted a return to the Arab fold.

On December 6, Burhan Ghalioun and six colleagues on the Syrian National Council were granted a meeting in Geneva with U.S. Secretary of State Hillary Clinton. The movement in American diplomacy had been glacial, given the violence that had engulfed Syria. This was not quite official recognition of the opposition, but the opponents of the regime were glad to have it. The reports from Homs, now the epicenter of this struggle, were particularly bleak: at least fifty people were reported killed, and the Syrian Observatory for Human Rights said thirty-six victims kidnapped from anti-regime neighborhoods had been tortured and then dumped in a square on the fault line between the Sunni and Alawi quarters. Stuart Ramsay, a veteran British reporter for Sky News, managed to report secretly from Homs. He was smuggled into the city by activists and members of the Free Syrian Army. Ramsay found the precedent for what he had seen: Homs was akin to Sarajevo under siege. He brought out of Homs heartbreaking footage of women and children scurrying for cover and running for their lives. A Friday prayer carried the despair of Homs: the beseeching of God growing more passionate and strident as people prayed for a deliverance they suspected might never come. There were boys in their teens, and their prayer had in it, I thought, a mix of needed belief and a knowingness that they were on their own.

"They're not my forces," Bashar al-Assad said when asked about the severity of the crackdown against the protesters in an interview December 7 with the American celebrity journalist

Barbara Walters. "They are military forces that belong to the government. I don't own them. I'm president. I don't own the country. No government kills its own people unless it is led by a crazy
person." The ruler who showed up for the interview was a well-
spoken, educated young man. He had never issued orders for a
crackdown. Some mistakes were made, but there was no deliberate policy of the sort. He felt no guilt, he said, because he had
done nothing wrong. It was vintage Bashar al-Assad, this alternation between light and darkness that had become the hallmark of
the man. He was the master of the regime, but it wasn't his. The
renowned oppositionist Michel Kilo, in an appropriately titled
opinion column—"What Does the President Know?"—offered a
scathing rebuttal of this willful innocence. Assad's was a one-man
regime, he said. He is the president, the commander of the armed
forces, the head of the popular organization, "the first artisan, the
first laborer, the first journalist, the first doctor, the first engineer,
the first peasant, the first artist, etc. Finally he is also the first
informer who looks into and is aware of all matters, large and
small. . . . A few months earlier, he claimed that he met 1,180
delegations who brought him news of the problems of the land."
It was odd, Kilo said, that the man who holds in his hands all the
threads of politics, security, the economy, and the media now
feigned such innocence. Kilo recalled an incident that had taken
place only weeks earlier. Assad had been asked if he intended to
bequeath the presidency to his son, now 10 years of age. He said
it was up to the boy, but that he would advise the son to forge
the most extensive relations with Syrian society. The country was
awash with violence, yet the regime's "first man" would not own
up to it.

Days after this broadcast, the United Nations Human Rights
Council would recommend referring Syria and its ruler to the

International Criminal Court in The Hague. If the aim of the interview was to show a Western audience the well-mannered man at the helm of the Damascus regime, the effort had been a failure. The killings in Homs and the disclosure by the United Nations that 5,000 Syrians had been killed thus far and thousands were still missing had overtaken this public relations gambit.

There were grimmer estimates on the scale of the bloodshed. Avaaz, a British-based advocacy group, put the fatalities at 6,200. Four hundred children were among the dead, more than 600 had died under torture, and the toll on the security forces was just short of a thousand. The ruler's choices had narrowed and crystallized: the defeat of the rebellion, exile for himself and his family, or a fate similar to that of Libya's Qaddafi. The economy had shrunk by 30 percent, the Syrian pound had collapsed, and the country was running out of fuel oil. The regime's darkening prospects had led it to accept a team of monitors from the Arab League. But the violence was intensified—such was the view held by the regime of the authority of the Arab League. In one such outburst of violence, (December 20–22), more than 160 people were killed—army defectors, activists, and ordinary men and women caught in the crossfire. The village of Kafr Oweid, in the hinterland of the town of Idlib and by the border with Turkey, was in for a particularly cruel punishment. More than 100 of its people were killed in the course of a single day. The imam of the village was beheaded, and his head was hung in the entrance of his mosque. This was not a regime out to "engage" its rebellious population.

Hitherto, Damascus itself—as distinct from its restive outskirts—had been spared. But on December 23, as the Arab League monitors had made their appearance, two car bombs exploded outside government offices in a heavily guarded part of the city. More than forty people were killed. The authorities were quick to announce that the bombings "had the fingerprints of Al Qaeda all over." The timing was odd: a city under a draconian security network had been hit as the Arab monitors had arrived. For the regime, this was dramatic proof that terrorists and armed groups were at work in Syria. A regime functionary could not wait: "We said it from the beginning, this is terrorism," the deputy foreign minister said. "They are killing the army and civilians." The regime's opponents would not be swayed: they were sure that a ruling cabal with a history of cruelty and dirty tricks had staged this operation to throw the Arab monitors off balance. Beirut and Baghdad had had their own bitter experience with car bombs and suicide operations. No one ever knew with precision who pulled off these grim deeds. The evidence was always circumstantial, the domain of conjecture. This regime was not above suspicion. In the catalogue of its crimes, this was a petty affair. Al Qaeda had not targeted Syria; indeed Al Qaeda terrorists had made their way to Iraq courtesy of the regime in Damascus. The "jihad" in Iraq had subsided, and the chickens had come home to roost. The Syrian rulers had befriended militants and die-hards—who had nothing but loathing for the regime and its Alawi masters.

A religious cover was given the regime's version of these bombings. Shaykh Muhammad Said al-Buti, from his perch in the Umayyad Mosque in Damascus, cast subtlety aside. "This was the gift of Burhan Ghalioun and his comrades to Syria," the cleric said, referring to the head of the National Syrian Council and his colleagues. "Are the blindfolds now removed from the eyes of the Arab League representatives to see who is the killer and who's the victim?"

The lines were drawn—and they of course divided the religious class as well. On the other side of Shaykh Buti, from Al-Hassan

Mosque in the Midan quarter of Old Damascus, was Karim al-Rajeh. The widely respected cleric—the chief of the country's Koran reciters, a man in his eighties—weighed in on the malady in the land. In a widely circulated statement that made its way to YouTube, he called on President Assad to "submit to reason and to stop the killings and the torture inflicted on the Syrian people." The country had slipped out of the "rule of reason," the cleric said. Damascus had become an "insane asylum," he added. "Syria is more powerful than anyone who would claim to rule it. The blood of a Muslim is more precious than all the presidencies and high offices. When you are a servant of Allah, all will be called upon to submit to you. But when you violate Allah's command, all those who had submitted to you before will be enjoined to rebel against you. I want to say to the regime that torture and other misdeeds will not silence the people. This way, we are only adding the fuel to the fire, and this fire will spread, take in the entire country. The people are mightier than the state." The old cleric had been banned from preaching in his mosque, but he had found a way to be heard.

The regime had effectively stalled and played for time. Though it had something of an insurance policy at the United Nations Security Council—the support of Russia and China—it still was wary of "internationalizing" this conflict. As the Syrian rulers insisted that Libya had been a case apart, they were determined to keep this struggle in the Arab councils of power. This was an arena they knew and mastered.

By the appearance of things, Damascus did not believe that the Arab political order had changed in the course of a tumultuous year that played havoc with its settled ways. Sure enough, there were new governments in Tunisia and Libya that sympathized with the Syrian uprising, but Damascus stuck to its playbook. It would run out the clock in the hope that the forces of the

opposition would tire of hurling themselves against an entrenched
regime willing to use all means necessary to survive. Men find
new liberties and a new license when they shed old, restraining
myths, and the regime and its masters were now stripped of the
old myths. Bashar al-Assad now knew that the act that he and
his polished wife had pulled off—the promise of a new beginning
by a young, modern couple—had collapsed. No foreign luminar-
ies were calling on him, and even the Russians and the Chinese
were now given to muffled demands for reform of his regime. On
the other side of the respectable order of nations, he and his ruling cabal found the brutality that comes to rogue states that free
themselves of the shackles of normalcy. It's a game we play,
Bashar al-Assad told interviewer Barbara Walters, when she
asked him about the United Nations and the rebuke he had
received from its Human Rights Council. Syria was a member
state in that organization, the ruler said, but it was all a con and
a game—a cynicism there to put Old Man Assad to shame.

The cat-and-mouse game was being played to perfection. The
Arab monitors—all fifty of them—were on the scene as the bombardment of Homs continued. The city was under siege, entire
neighborhoods without food, electricity, or water. It did not bode
well for this Arab League mission that it was headed by Lt. Gen.
Mohammed al-Dabi, a Sudanese military man and security officer who was a protégé of Sudan's President Omar Bashir. The
Sudanese ruler was subject to an arrest warrant by the International Criminal Court. Dabi, a man of Bashir's security services,
was no angel. He had carried out many assignments in Darfur for
his political master. His did not have the right pedigree for a
mission of this kind. The assignment must have come his way
because the Syrians insisted on a chief observer from a regime
friendly to them.

General Dabi had not disappointed the authorities in Damascus. He had gone to Homs, but he didn't see anything "frightening" in that city, he said. By the Darfur standard the statement was accurate, but there had been suffering aplenty in Homs. YouTube was loaded with evidence of great cruelty. There were old Soviet T72 tanks shelling the Baba Amr neighborhood, and there were men standing amid the ruin of their alleys, pointing out where family members and neighbors had fallen. They were beseeching the powers of the world, and God Almighty, for deliverance. The rage at the Arab League alternated with pleas for help. The body of a 5-year-old boy was shown the monitors, presented as a young "martyr." On a YouTube video, the monitors could be seen asking for calm, as one of them touched the dead boy's head and closed his eyes. When the monitors headed next to Deraa and the outskirts of Damascus, thousands had turned out for a mass rally and the security forces had fired on the crowd. No great deference was shown these monitors—and it's no wonder they came to be dubbed the Arab spectators. It was idle to hope that the Arab League had much to offer this embattled rebellion. Once again, popular wisdom—plain and unadorned, schooled by bitter experience—caught the truth of this conflict. A placard, held aloft by a group of Homsi women, put the diplomatic-speak to shame. "All doors are closed, except yours, Oh God." Ankara had not sent troops across the border, NATO planes had not turned up over the skies of Homs, and these Arab League monitors were of no consequence. The killings went on under their gaze. The Tunisian and Egyptian despots had called it quits after a fortnight of troubles. Qaddafi had held on, but his madness and erratic ways had doomed him. Qaddafi's brutal "honesty" at the end did him in. He was forthright about the terror he had in mind for the rebels in Benghazi who had dared challenge his rule. He had the world's undivided attention when he said his forces were on their way to Benghazi to hunt down his enemies, house by house, neighborhood by neighborhood, alleyway by alleyway. He had shredded all ambiguity, and a small-scale Rwanda appeared imminent. The powers in Paris, London, and Washington had been jolted into action.

The cold-blooded ruler in Damascus, his tyranny anchored in a minority sect, and a merciless security apparatus had been excessively careful with his image and utterances. There was brutality by the vigilantes and the security forces, and talk of "reform" by the master of the regime. There was no way of knowing whether the rebellion would have started had its leaders and foot soldiers known what hellish struggle awaited them. The regime had presented them with the cruelest of choices: the fearsome tyranny or this time of untold suffering.

When this rebellion was still in its early months, Patrick Seale, a British political historian and commentator who had written Hafez al-Assad's standard biography in 1988, laid out the balance of raw power at the heart of this fight: Damascus had not rebelled, the army had not defected, the economy had not collapsed, the regime was weak, and the opposition weaker. As the conflict was closing in on its first year, the Seale yardstick still held. There were stirrings in Damascus, but no full-scale rebellion. There were army defectors with a small piece of liberated geography in Homs, but the instruments of repression were more or less intact—fear had kept the army obedient to the regime. (There was one interesting defection. A young lieutenant, Abdul Razzaq Tlas, willingly revealed his identity to an unnamed reporter: he was a nephew of General Mustafa Tlas, a loyalist of Hafez al-Assad, a pillar of the regime, and defense minister for well over three decades. The young man was unapologetic. His soldier's honor, he said, would not permit him to kill unarmed civilians.) To be sure, the economy was reeling and the regime was staring into the abyss of huge deficits. It was even speaking of financing its operations by going back to the business classes and merchants who had done well by the economic policy of the preceding decade and securing a "refund" from them—through new legislation of course. The relative balance of forces between the regime and the opposition was hard to gauge. The regime had lost its *haiba* (its aura), the fear accorded it by a hitherto obedient population, but it was still holding on. The opposition had grown wider and larger. It had gained some traction on the regional and international stage, but its leaders were in exile and trying to overthrow the regime from venues in Geneva, Istanbul, Brussels, and Tunis.

As 2011 drew to a close, foreign intervention had not materialized. In December, Frederick Hof, a State Department official with a clever turn of phrase, had described the Bashar regime as a "dead man walking." There was policy analysis in that statement, but wishful thinking as well. American officials would have loved to see this regime collapse from its own weight, sparing them hard, uncomfortable choices. There were reports that the Obama administration was considering its "options" and readying plans to aid the opposition to Bashar. But these very same reports spoke of dissent within the administration, of concerns about the unity and the goals of the Syrian opposition—a replay of the reluctant American commitment to Libya. The president of the United States had by word and deed given away his aversion to costly and divisive military engagements abroad. He was ceding strategic space and interests in the Muslim world. His foreign policy plank was circumscribed. On December 8, he rebutted the charge that he pursued appeasement abroad: "Ask Osama bin

Laden and the 22 out of 30 top Al Qaeda leaders who have been taken off the field whether I engage in appeasement. Or whoever's left out there, ask them about that." This president would do counterterrorism, but a plunge into big contests in complicated places was not for him. In all fairness, he had not made promises to the Syrians that he did not keep.

In the nature of things, the opposition took the onset of 2012 as a turning point of consequence. It vowed that the year would witness the fall of the regime. The great stalemate was not broken in 2011. The protesters, as noted repeatedly in this narrative, had given each Friday a name, a theme. All told, forty-two Fridays had come and gone in the course of the rebellion in 2011. Bashar had not made his way to some exile in Russia or Iran, and the opposition wasn't about to surrender and return to the obedience of days past. It had been assumed by the opposition that the regime would fall during the holy month of Ramadan—corresponding with the month of August—in 2011. That hope had been in vain. The regime and its opponents had dug in for a long fight. Each side had shown the other the measure of its determination to prevail. Countries are rarely in play, but Syria as a whole was being contested. It would simplify things to depict this fight as the determined struggle of the Sunni majority to retrieve its world from a minoritarian domination. But that was the truth that finally animated, and shaped, this struggle.

The regime's cruelty and staying power had gone a long way toward altering the worldview of its opponents. More candor about the need for Western intervention could be heard in their utterances. In the opening days of January 2012, Samir Nashar, an executive board member of the Syrian National Council, took it upon himself to state what was on the minds of so many others caught up in this struggle. The majority of his peers in the opposition, he said, agree on the need for international military intervention. But "they might not be brave enough to express it openly. The people on the ground are growing restless and desperate." The opposition had been hoping for a military coup against the regime, "but there are no guarantees such a coup would occur." Nashar punctured the myth that Syrian opinion was opposed to Western help: "The vast majority of the Syrians I know were completely supportive of what NATO did in Libya." Several generations of Syrians had grown up on a diet of militant nationalism. This searing rebellion had taught them that that political tradition was a swindle, an instrument of the dictators, an alibi for the ruin that had settled upon their country. Pity the Syrians, they had been raised on the legend that their country was the "beating heart of Arabism." They woke up amidst the debris, and this squalid kleptocracy was what they had gotten in the bargain. Those oppositionists maintaining that their ranks were filled with those pining for foreign intervention were vindicated. Friday, January 6, was given an honest name: International Protection Is Our Demand.

In their defiance, the protesters could maintain that time was on their side. In truth, time took no side in this fight, for the opposition, too, was tested by the passage of time. Moncef Marzouki, the newly chosen Tunisian president and a prominent and credible campaigner for human rights who backed this Syrian rebellion to the hilt, expressed a legitimate concern about its direction. The revolution, he said, had become sectarian, weaponized, and internally fragmented. This was a sympathizer's testimony, and those caught up in this rebellion knew the truth of his judgment.

A testimony by Jean Clement Jeanbart, the archbishop of Aleppo's Greek Roman Catholic Church, exposed the religious fault lines in a deeply divided country. His forum was an interview he gave to the French daily *Le Figaro*, and his remarks were amplified by the organs of the regime. "Christians don't trust extremist Sunni power. We fear the dogmatic Muslim Brothers." His bet was on the ruler: "Despite the unrest, you have to give Assad a chance. The regime has the support of the minorities." For this clergyman, as it had been for Christian clergy and laymen alike, the cautionary tale was what had transpired in Iraq—the flight of so many Christians after the fall of Saddam. Nor had the archbishop been comforted by the aftermath of the revolutions of the Arab Spring. "The fall of regimes that are seen as dictatorial could lead to civil war, of which the Christians could be the main victims."

Archbishop Jeanbart was sure of his numbers: the regime had the support of minorities, he said, and were one to add the Alawites, Christians, Druze, Kurds, Ismailis, Baath Party members, and the Sunni traders of Damascus and Aleppo, "you've probably got more than 50 percent behind Bashar." The defense of the minorities and of the "secularism" of this divided country was the central plank of the regime. Now the argument would be advanced by a shrewd and supremely political clergyman. Jeanbart had a trail behind him. He had spoken in this fashion before, and he was no friend of populist movements. But he was now more blunt than ever. It didn't matter whether these remarks were freely given, or if the regime had pressed for so open a declaration of loyalty. The unity of the country was, at best, a pretense.

If the opposition was divided—those inside versus those in exile, those hoping for international protection and those unalterably opposed to it, those determined to overthrow the regime and those who held out hope for deliverance through negotiations with the rulers—the regime, at least its inner core, was possessed of brutal clarity. On January 10, more than six months after his last oration to the country, Bashar al-Assad turned up at Damascus University for a speech that left no ambiguity about where he stood. This was his fourth speech since the eruption of the troubles, and it was a meandering performance that lasted an hour and a half—twenty-five minutes longer, it was noted, than a speech in the same mold by the Libyan dictator, Muammar el-Qaddafi. He was not going anywhere, he said. He had come to power through "the will of the people," and he would give up only through the will of the people. He needed no advice from the Arab states sitting in judgment of his regime. "Those states that counsel us to reform have no knowledge of democracy whatsoever. They resemble a physician advising others to quit smoking with a cigarette dangling from his lips." The Arab League has no standing suspending Syria's membership, for when its members do so "they suspend the very Arabism of the League." This Arab League, he adds, was but a reflection of the debased Arab condition, for there were regimes that inwardly supported Syria, but outwardly stood against it, because they have lost their sovereignty and independent will. He heaped scorn on unnamed Arab countries—clearly the Gulf states, with Qatar at the head of the pack no doubt— that have no grand history, but attempt to purchase it with money. He was ready to negotiate with the opposition, he said, even with those who "committed deeds of terrorism in the 1970s and 1980s"—a clear reference to the Muslim Brotherhood. "The fog has lifted. It was no longer possible to falsify events," for it was clear now that Syria was engulfed by conspiracies. There were foreign conspirators, but Arab conspirators as well, waging an unprecedented campaign, through countless television channels and tens of Internet sites and newspapers.

Pop psychologists stepped forth: it was said that the man in the eye of the storm had a compulsion to prove his toughness. He had been the dutiful, quiet son to his father, the son good at studies. He had two tougher, more "manly" brothers, both military men: Basel, the older one lost to that car accident, and his younger brother Maher in command of the regime's elite forces. The rebellion had given him his chance, and he had seized it. He would fight and kill for his father's bequest. His mother, Anisa Makhlouf, a reputed woman of steel, was still alive. She had been by Hafez al-Assad's side for four decades, a close confidante. Her advice to Bashar was to play by his father's rules and defend the dynasty.

The defiant speech had not sufficed; the next day, Bashar turned up at a mass rally in Damascus's Umayyad Square. His wife and two of his children accompanied him. He had not done that sort of thing before, and the festive occasion and the delirious crowd were dazzlingly choreographed. The opposition dismissed this as a rigged audience with government employees and shabiha making an obligatory appearance. But the message was clear: he was hunkered down for a long fight and promised that victory over the "terrorists" and the naysayers was near.

Defectors had begun to provide more detail about the workings of the regime. Shaykh Abduljalil al-Said, a young, highly placed cleric and the head of the information office of Mufti Ahmad Hassoun, made his way to Istanbul in mid-January. He spoke of a divided and troubled (Sunni) religious establishment. There were many clerics, he said, who had no faith in the government or its supplicant ulama. He had worked directly with the mufti and depicted him as an eager man of the regime who took part in the deliberations of the security organs and who insisted that the Assad rule was there to stay. The mufti was "obsessed with power," he said. This was no man of religion, but an intensely ambitious and worldly man steeped in corruption and compromises. The entire religious institution was under constant surveillance, Shaykh Said observed. The Friday sermons are closely monitored, and anyone who deviates from the regime's instructions is sent home, "never to return." A tight group of a dozen or so senior clerics oversee the religious institution, its charities, and the principal mosques. But the authority of this "religious pyramid" does not extend to the Alawis and their religious leaders. The mufti of the Alawis is a law unto himself, and he does not defer to Mufti Hassoun or the minister of religious endowments. Shaykh Said had broken with the official religious guild in the hope that others would be encouraged to do so. He wanted to acquit himself "before God and the nation that will show no mercy toward those who stand with the criminals." The regime was not slow in responding to him. Soon after he had taken that step, his father and oldest brother were arrested.

THIS REBELLION opened up the central question as to the fate of the Alawis—and with it perhaps the unity of the Syrian nation-state. Among the Arab rebellions of 2011, this was unique to Syria: Tunisia and Egypt were old national communities with a settled sense of belonging. Libya had a cleavage between Benghazi and Tripoli, but there was no ruling caste in Libya, no dominant community. Syria, so proud of its statehood, so militant as to its place among the states of the region, was riven by essential fault lines—no doubt a factor in the official belligerence about Syria's pride and its nationhood. The revolt of 2011 led straight back to the founding of the state and its emergence in the 1930s and 1940s. Colonial fiat played a role in drawing the boundaries of the state—the nurturing by France of the communal aspirations of the Alawis and the Druze, and then their abandonment. The French had waged war against the urban elite, broke the (Sunni) cities in the 1920s, and then gave in to them a generation later. The "unionists" had won a state that herded the Alawis, the Druze, and the Kurds into a polity ruled from Damascus with a privileged role for Aleppo, Hama, and Homs.

The unity had backfired when the Alawis upended the old order and hijacked some of that order's cherished claims: the struggle against Israel, the revisionist bid for Lebanon, and the insistence that these Alawi soldiers would retrieve Alexandretta from the Turks and the Golan Heights from Israel. Thus did the Alawi schismatics pose as the warriors of Arabism. With his keen eye for history's complications, Henry A. Kissinger saw in those pan-Arab furies what the master of the Syrian regime, Hafez al-Assad, so skillfully embodied—and manipulated. "Damascus is at one and the same time the fount of modern Arab nationalism and the exhibit of its frustrations. Syrian history alternates achievement with catastrophe. The injustice of foreigners is burned deep into the Syrian soul." If the Damascus Arab nationalists were aggrieved by what the West had done to their imagined glory, Assad, a child of the mountain, would outdo them in that sense of belligerent grief and betrayal. From Kissinger again: "Assad said to me that Syria had been betrayed before World War I by Turkey, after it by Britain and France, and more recently by the United States which had created the State of Israel."

In retrospect, Hafez al-Assad had suspended, but never resolved, the feuds of Syria's communities. These feuds and warring identities were placed in a freezer, as it were. Assad was to Syria what Josip Broz Tito was to Yugoslavia. Tito had been a formidable political player. By sheer personality and skill he had held together an impossible country. Hailing from a mixed Croat-Slovene marriage, he had balanced the competing nationalisms of that most gerrymandered of nation-states. He both satisfied and kept in check Serbian nationalism, created something of a balance between the Serbs and the Croats, and sheltered the smaller nationalisms. His death in 1980 was the starting gun for the plunge into political warfare. Before long, the constituent parts of Yugoslavia would fight for and secure their own statehood. In the fashion of Tito, Hafez al-Assad had given his country three decades of unity, the sort of cohesion that was not destined to last. He had been enormously skilled in the way he had deployed the Alawis: they were the inner core of his regime, its last resort. But he was the master of the realm, not the Alawis as a community. He knew that he could summon them in a moment of peril, as he did during that troubled time (1979–1982). But he aspired to something larger and more exalted, a role for himself as a pan-Arab leader in a city of consequence. The diplomacy of Anwar al-Sadat (the journey to Jerusalem in 1977, the peace of Camp David, and the choice in Cairo of securing a place for Egypt in the Pax Americana) had left Assad as the standard-bearer of militant Arab nationalism, and he seized it with relish. It saw him to the end of his rule, which he bequeathed to his political inheritor. Pan-Arabism helped paper over the Alawi background.

The rebellion of 2011 raised, once again, the thorny question of Alawi identity, the Alawi "ownership" of the regime. Nearly a year into the killings, Ali Asa'ad Watfa, an Alawi scholar and a professor of education at Kuwait University for well over a decade, gave this question a sustained scrutiny in an essay appropriately titled "The Alawi Community in the Dock: A Sociological

Reading." Watfa was a French-educated academic, broadly liberal and secularist in outlook, and keen to stay away from the feuds of his native country. He was apologetic about sectarianism being the starting point of his analysis. "I am neither of the regime, nor of the opposition. I am away from my country, and have refrained from such discussions." But the issue of Syrian violence could no longer be avoided. Watfa asks the right questions: Why haven't the Alawis joined the rebellion? What accounts for their refusal to do so? Do they, as a community, bear responsibility for this criminal regime? These questions are pertinent, he conceded, because the head of the regime and his family are Alawis and because a high percentage of the officer corps and crack brigades hail from the ruler's community.

Alawi opinion, Watfa wants it understood, had been dubious of Assad's assumption of the presidency. Conscious of their minoritarian status, most Alawis did not want the sins of the regime attributed to the community as a whole. Furthermore, to the extent that Alawi sentiment at the time could be gauged, their preference in that power struggle in 1970 was decidedly in favor of Assad's rival, General Salah Jadid. The Assad regime had chosen loyalists among the Alawis, Watfa adds, as it did in other communities—the willingness to accept and defend the corporate interests of the regime was the precondition of recruitment. In an economically desperate community, it had not been difficult to recruit among the Alawis. The latter joined the armed forces out of necessity.

For Watfa, this ruling regime was not the dominion of one community over the others. It was a multisectarian enterprise, a merchant-military complex that functioned to the advantage of the privileged classes. The regime had broken with its early economic populism, and the beneficiaries of this new system were

Sunni and Christian interests. The Alawis, the Druze, and the Kurds are outside the charmed circle. This kleptocracy was an enemy of the poor. In Watfa's rendition, the Alawis bear historical handicaps they have never been able to shed. They are the sole community in the country without its own courts and laws that pertain to personal status. All matters of marriage, property, and inheritance are decided in accord with Sunni jurisprudence. In the myth of the Assad dictatorship, the regime is a protector of the minorities, but it had done little to advance the interests of the forgotten poor.

The Assads had "militarized" the Alawis, turning them into a Praetorian guard. And this, Watfa notes, came at a terrible price. The educational standards among Alawi youth had collapsed, and schools had been emptied as young Alawis were recruited into special battalions. The wretched quarters at the entrance of the big cities that are home to frustrated and impoverished soldiers are a testament to the sordid lot of these soldiers. No wealth had accrued for the Alawis as a whole. A new "feudal" class had arisen among the Alawis, and their big villas dot the landscape in their ancestral villages, but the widespread poverty had not been ameliorated. The shabiha are on the lookout. "Punishment inside the sect is a thousand times worse than the punishment meted out to other communities." In the Alawi coastal towns, the shabiha are gangsters who live off and terrorize Alawis without means or official pull. Watfa knew *ahl al-Sahel* (the people of the coast). They were not sectarian, and they had always yearned for a "common life" with their neighbors.

Watfa had given the issue of Alawi ownership of the regime a mighty try. In the manner of a good, eager advocate, he had done his best to exonerate his community. There was a good deal of truth in his exposition. He was right in his assertion that the

Sunni elite had done well by the regime, all the more so in the
"open" economy that Bashar had opted for. And doubtless he was
right in the reminder that the Alawis as a community had not
prospered under the dictatorship. But the special pleading in his
exposition is obvious. In the Syria of the Assads, Alawis have
done well by official employment in the public sector, by favoritism in access to water in agricultural areas, and by the usual
opportunities for pillage and extortion granted men in uniform.
Public expenditures in the Assad years gave the Alawis of the
coast an edge they had never had. In the Baniyas oil refinery
the Alawis had a huge advantage in employment, and this fed the
frustrations and anger of the Sunnis of that city. A university had
opened in Latakia; state patronage had been kind to the Alawis.
For all the advantages of Aleppo and Damascus merchants, the
assertion that this was at heart a Sunni regime is patently false.

The dexterity that Watfa exhibited could yet find its usages.
When the accounts are done between the Sunni majority and the
Alawis, the proposition that the Alawis did not rule Syria and
that the House of Assad was the guilty party could be the way out
of terrible bloodletting. A regime long in the saddle implicates all.
After four decades of tyranny, no one can claim to have clean
hands. Tyranny is skilled that way; it makes sure that all within
its reach are sullied.

There hovers over the discussion of Alawi domination, and its
coming apart, the question of the territorial integrity of the Syrian
state. Alawi separatism has always been one of these scripts held
out for Syria. In a moment of peril, when the power of the Alawis
is broken, that community would beat a retreat to its home in
Jebel Ansariyah and the coast. There, they would make a stand
and leave a scorched earth behind them. An "artificial" state

would thus be undone. This future would have finality and symmetry going for it. But in truth it is unlikely to come to pass. The most improbable of states—contrived and conceived by mapmakers who knew neither the lands nor the peoples whose fate they determined—have managed to survive. The international system of states conspires to perpetuate such states on grounds of convenience. On Syria's western border there is Lebanon—designed by the French in 1920 and the setting of intermittent local and regional wars ever since, it was the home of several communities with clashing histories. If any nation-state were to have its borders rectified and its membership in the order of states revoked, Lebanon should have come to that end long ago. But still the country endures even as its statehood is tested and powers beyond toy with it. To Syria's east there is Iraq, the most "invented" of states. Baghdad had conceded "autonomy"—virtual independence—for Kurdistan, and the schism between the Sunnis in the west and the Shia in Baghdad and farther south is as deep as could be imagined. Yet Iraq as a nation-state survives. Iraqis go to the edge of the precipice and pull back. They fight within the borders of a national home and over the country and its identity and oil. Convenience has taken on the quality of permanence.

Consider as well the last of the Arab states that border Syria, the Hashemite kingdom of Jordan. This was the state that Winston Churchill claimed to have created in a single afternoon, a buffer state set up for a Hashemite prince in search of a domain of his own—Abdullah Ibn Hussein. Prince Abdullah had wanted a reign in Damascus, and pined for that city for the bulk of his political life. But he made peace with Jordan, a consolation prize, and described himself as a "falcon trapped in a canary's cage." That improbable principality survived Abdullah's assassination in

1951 and knew nearly a half-century of relative stability under his remarkable grandson, King Hussein. Waves of Palestinian refugees swamped Jordan—in 1948, 1967, and in 1990–1991 from Kuwait—testing its coherence and the loyalties of its population. The region needed Jordan, as did those who came to identify themselves as Jordanians. Obituaries of this kingdom have been written time and again, and the obituarists have been proved wrong.

There is no likelihood of reviving the state of the Alawites or the government of Latakia—the two names the French gave to the Alawite territory. The vision of the Alawi barons and security officers quitting Damascus and taking up agricultural work in villages where the land had long been annulled is pure fantasy. Alawis quit the land for a good reason: it would not sustain them nor satisfy their material needs and ambitions. Hafez al-Assad was buried in his ancestral village of Qardaha, though he had been schooled in Latakia and then the military academy in Homs, with the presidential palace in Damascus as his destination. Qardaha's supreme gift to him was the elemental recognition that life could not be had within its confines.

There is no place for an Alawi state, as such an entity could not make its way in the world. In the Alawi homeland, the mountain has its back to the coast, and the coastal towns have their back turned toward the sea. When the Alawis of the coast sought a viable world, they headed toward the cities of the interior— toward Homs, but above all to Damascus. They sought state power and patronage rather than the opportunities of commerce and the sea. The differences with the people of the coast in Lebanon were profound: the Mediterranean shaped the worldview of the Lebanese, the sea beckoned, and from the sea came an appetite for risk and commerce. The great historian Arnold Toynbee, in his monumental *A Study of History*, noted the profound differences in temperament between the people of Mount Lebanon and those who inhabited Alawi lands. Toynbee spoke of a subtle force at work in the affairs of men; he called it the stimulus of pressure. The people of Mount Lebanon and the Lebanese coast were driven, those in the Alawi territory less so. "In the light of the local precedents it looks as though the Lebanese had been stimulated to emulate the Phoenicians by the barrenness of their native mountain, while the agreeableness of the Jebel Ansariyah has inveighed the Nusayris into vegetating in a Philistine sloth."

Alawis can't live off the sea or slice off a piece of Syria and there make their stand. The habits of capitalism take centuries to develop and transmit. If anything, the decades of dictatorship had given the Alawis little social capital that they can draw on. Their military power had been used to buttress their wealth at home, and to draw on the aid that the Arab states of the Peninsula and the Gulf had made available to the Syrian state. An Alawi entity of some 2 million people that hurls itself against the power of Damascus and of Arabs beyond has no chance of survival. A military base in Tartus could be hired out to the Russians; this would enable Russia to pose as a great naval power, but much more than a derelict Russian base is needed to sustain a viable communal home. The true solution is much messier than the neat scenario of partition. The Alawis who made their way to Homs and Damascus will have to stay put. Life being what it is, a price will have to be paid for the transgressions and liberties taken in the course of an "unnatural" dominion. The Alawis and those who will come to govern a new Syrian polity will have to draw up a pact of their own. For the Alawis, their place is destined to be somewhere equidistant between the subjugation of old and the power that came their way in the four decades of the dictatorship.

That dreaded past had been unjust to the Alawis, the sectarian dictatorship both unnatural and cruel to the vast majority of the population. It will not be easy for Syrians to find the way out of the cauldron of their recent history.

FOR WELL OVER TEN MONTHS, the regime's power had kept Damascus out of the turmoil. By late January 2012, the rebellion engulfed the satellite towns around the capital. Thirty miles away, the resort town of Rankhous had risen; its people had fled for safety when the security forces swept in. Douma, nine miles from Damascus, had caught the spirit of the rebellion earlier and was the scene of intermittent clashes. Arbeen, a mere four miles from the Old City, had stirred. So had Zabadani, by the border with Lebanon twenty miles away. It had been the claim of the rulers that they were the guardians of order, and now the once-mighty state had lost its grip.

Aleppo, rebuked and mocked by the rebels for its submission, wanted its honor redeemed. The Aleppines wanted it known that they had been into the rebellion all along and that the University of Aleppo was the "university of the revolution." There had been the good and honorable Ibrahim al-Salqini, the mufti of Aleppo, who had died in early September. The Aleppine activists insisted that his funeral procession had turned into a demonstration against the regime, that pictures of the ruler had been burned, and that the mourners had called for a trial of Bashar for his crimes against the Syrian people. Aleppo had been misunderstood, its defenders said. It had never been a pillar of the dictatorship. Other places that had paid dearly for the defiance were not convinced, but they drew comfort from the small deeds of

Aleppine defiance. They took it as a herald that perhaps the crafty Aleppines were reading the wind.

It so happened that February 2012 marked the thirtieth anniversary of the Hama massacres. Grief had not let go of Syria. But this new rebellion differed from the earlier one in an important way. There were the camera phones and the YouTube videos. One YouTube posting paid tribute to Hama's sorrow. It was a visual presentation of the destruction that had befallen the bereaved city, set to music of lament and heartbreak. It made for a powerful impression—a city in ruins as though a foreign army had battered it without mercy. Another posting bespoke of the banality of evil. It had Rifaat al-Assad, Hafez's younger brother, now in exile, as a preening, uncomprehending man, slightly tacky in appearance. He was the one who had led the assault on Hama. He now spoke of that time as though all should be forgiven and forgotten. He spoke as a man of the state and of order. He rebuked those who would speak of Hama without the burden of knowledge. Rifaat was there. The *Ikhwan*, the Muslim Brotherhood, had been subversive and cruel, he said. And their leaders had issued fatwas declaring the Alawis, the Druze, and the Ismailis *kuffar* (infidels). The Muslim Brotherhood had never given the Baathist "revolution" a chance. They had struck against it as early as 1964, one year after its capture of power. There was pride and moral obtuseness in the man's remarks and demeanor. Dreams of power never die. It was known that this man, Bashar's uncle, had presented himself as an alternative to his nephew.

In this amply documented and photographed rebellion, there were endless scenes of slaughter and heartbreak. From Homs, in a video from late January, an old woman is pleading for the Arab cavalry to come to the rescue and telling them that the Sunnis are being massacred. In a video on January 30, also from Homs, an entire family, murdered and bearing horrific signs of torture, is displayed—a child still holding on to his mother's hair. The camera is intrusive here. It spares nothing and makes no allowance for squeamishness. This is not Hollywood, this is not a film, a young man says, as the camera closes in on the victims. We have tired of taking pictures, he says. We will put down the camera and take up the gun. An older man prays that the same horror that befell Syria's children be visited on the Russians and the Chinese, who had stood by the dictatorship.

In the chancelleries and the diplomatic corridors, there were confident predictions that this regime could not last. For those caught in its grip, those assertions offered no solace. Both the regime and those who had broken with it were betting that time was on their side. But time was not tipping its hand.

FEBRUARY 3 RECALLED the deep grief of Hama three decades earlier: Forgive Us Hama was the name given that Friday. There had always been a link between the twins Hama and Homs in the central plains. The Hamawis were known for their religious devotion and insularity, and Homsis were always the butt of jokes. Now, that intimate rivalry was underlined again. Hama had been "martyred" at the hands of the father, Homs now at the hands of the son. The son would throw at Homs the full might of his regime.

If the Homsis thought that the grief of the neighborhood of Baba Amr—the steady bombardment and the denial of medicine, food, and water—would draw the international cavalry to their side, February brought them steady disappointment. On February 4, the United Nations Security Council turned back a resolution calling on Bashar al-Assad to step down. Predictably, China and Russia had vetoed the resolution. Russia's foreign minister, Sergey Lavrov, would emerge as the principal defender of the Damascus dictatorship. That was Russia's moment, a way the Western democracies would be reminded that Russia was still a power among the nations.

There was resolve and genuine help offered by the friends of the Syrian regime—Russia, Iran, China, Hezbollah—and irresolution among the ranks of the democracies and the "moderate" Arab regimes. The latter gave away their ambivalence about the Syrian rebellion in late February, in Tunis, at a diplomatic gathering of what was dubbed the Friends of Syria. That convocation offered no relief for the battered country. The Tunisian hosts themselves proclaimed, on the eve of this meeting, that foreign military intervention in Syria was ruled out. Rescue hinged on American leadership, and this was not in the offing. An American president proud that he had shut down the Iraq war and pulled American troops out of that country was not about to engage American power on the other side of the Syria-Iraq frontier.

There was no shortage of alibis for American passivity: America did not know the protagonists and couldn't trust the Free Syrian Army, there was no United Nations Security Council resolution authorizing foreign intervention, and more. On February 26, Secretary of State Hillary Clinton, in an interview with CBS in Rabat, the Moroccan capital, all but took away any hope that there would be rescue for the Syrians. It was a stunning performance, a measure of the ability of power to avert its gaze from places in trouble. Why is it, she asked, that the people of Damascus and Aleppo had not rebelled? "Don't they know that their fellow Syrian men, women, and children are being slaughtered by their government? What are they going to do about it? When are

they going to start pulling the props out from under this illegiti-
mate government?" Syria wasn't the only place where people were
the victims of brutality, she said. Millions of people had been
killed in Eastern Congo, and the horror hadn't played out on
television. "There was no Skypeing from the jungles that were
the killing fields. You have to be very clear-eyed about what is
possible and what the consequences of anything you might wish
to do could be." It was morally and politically murky out there in
that Syrian landscape. Al Qaeda's leader, Ayman al-Zawahiri,
had weighed in with a broadcast on behalf of the opposition.
America could be caught, its chief diplomat said, on the side of
the devil. Secretary Clinton asked: "Are we supporting Al Qaeda
in Syria? Are we supporting Hamas in Syria?" The contrast with
Libya was part of this brief for abdication. There was no Benghazi
in Syria, and "you don't see uprisings in Syria the way you did in
Libya." There was immense human suffering in Syria, but the
stain was "on the honor of those security forces who are doing it."

This big fight in Syria reprised the arguments over Bosnia in
the early '90s. For thirty long, cruel months, while George H.W.
Bush and Bill Clinton stood idly by, the killings in Bosnia went
on and the Bosnians were subject to relentless terror. By that
Bosnian calendar and its scale of horrors, Syria still had a long
way to go. No Srebrenica had yet occurred in Syria. There was
and is in our world, tolerance aplenty for massive human
suffering.

"It was a revolution for a change. And now it became a battle
for existence," an unnamed activist posted on Twitter, on March
15—the rebellion's first anniversary. If there had been hope that
this rebellion would resemble the Tunisian and Egyptian upheavals, it had long been snuffed out. The human toll had risen, and
the numbers bespoke a regime determined to prevail at any cost.

The numbers, in a country largely inaccessible to the outside world, were an approximation. Where 700 people had been struck down in April 2011, 1,200 were killed in January 2012, and nearly 1,800 in February. By then the regime had sacked Homs and turned its wrath on Idlib. The conservative estimates of the United Nations put the toll at 8,000 victims, and all other estimates were much higher. Few Syrians believed the thousands unaccounted for would be seen again. The violence of the regime now made a mockery of any attempt to challenge it by peaceful means. Fayaz Sara, a writer and a journalist who had served two prison terms, was beaten up when he took part in a small demonstration in Damascus, on March 18. "The regime wants an opposition with a temperament like its own," said the 62-year-old Sara. Syrians had lost whatever illusions they had about the ease of overthrowing the dictatorship. When this all began, Syrians had looked on the violence that had befallen their neighbors in Lebanon and Iraq and wanted to believe that their country would be spared that carnage. They now knew better.

As the ruling cabal inflicted cruelty on the Syrians, it treated them to a display of the "banality of evil." Hackers had found their way to the emails of the first couple, a trove of some 3,000 messages between June 2011 and February 2012. The British paper *The Guardian* reported that it had received them from a source in the ruler's office. The emails made for an extraordinary reading. Bashar al-Assad could order a massive crackdown and still download his favorite songs on iTunes. There were young women in his entourage who swooned over him, delighted in his "strength, wisdom, and charisma, and of course his beauty." There was his father-in-law, the privileged cardiologist of Homsi background, from his London home, dispensing advice as to how the PR war could be fought. There was the ruler's wife shopping online for chandeliers and shoes, and looking for a fondue set and the latest installment of *Harry Potter*. The ruling husband and wife were certain they could ride out this storm. From the first lady came a message in December: "If we are strong together, we will overcome this together. I love you."

The barbarism and grief in Syria's cities and villages were kept out of this cocoon of privilege and denial. This was a "modern" tyranny that the late Hafez al-Assad could have never imagined.

CHAPTER TEN

Dreaming of Home:
A Note on the Exiles

I FOUND SHAYKH ANAS AL-AYROUT on the outskirts of Istanbul, in the shadow of a neighborhood mosque. This working-class district was at a great remove from the center of the city. I had read—and written—about this cleric, who had led the young people of the coastal town of Baniyas against the regime. In February 2012 I had come to Turkey to see, for myself, some of the Syrian oppositionists who had made Turkey their base. I was struck right away by the relative youth of the cleric. A handsome man and 40 years of age, he had a close-cropped beard and wore a leather jacket; there was no formalism of his guild. I could see why the young people of his town were drawn to him. He was a *khatib*, a prayer leader of his mosque; his father had been a celebrated religious figure, and Anas had taken up that calling. He had graduated from the College of the Shariah at Damascus University. It was easy to see him as a star among his peers. His powers of recall, ease with the language, and understanding of the political condition of his country were obvious. The Syrian coast was lost to him now, in this gritty neighborhood bound by barren hills.

Shaykh Anas had not wanted to plunge into the rebellion. He knew the special circumstances of Baniyas with its mixed population of Sunnis and Alawis, the proximity of the Alawi countryside, and the heavy presence of the security forces. But Baniyas had stirred in early 2011. He was proud of his hometown, and he insisted that its eruption had come right alongside that of Deraa's. A young man of 22, with a primary school education, had come to him and asked him to lead a demonstration against the regime. He hesitated and told the young man that he didn't think Baniyas was ready, that it would be demoralizing were they to call for a day of protest that would fizzle out. But this man of limited education had insisted, and he had quoted an Islamic maxim that Allah does not change a people's condition unless they themselves changed their ways. Several days later the young man returned with a group of his friends to appeal to Shaykh Anas. The shaykh relented, and the title of his *khutba*—his Friday sermon—that week was that injunction about people changing their own condition. He did not call for the overthrow of the regime. He talked of "reform"—the end of emergency rule, the release of detainees, the inequity that favored the Alawis. The oil refinery in Baniyas employed 4,000 workers, only a handful of them Sunnis. Alawis were brought in from as far away as Homs to fill the coveted refinery jobs, while the young Sunnis of Baniyas were shunted aside. There was also the matter of electricity costs—the Sunnis paid dearly for electricity while the Alawis paid nominal fees.

By Shaykh Anas's reckoning, another issue had enraged the conservative town of Baniyas: coeducation. The government had decreed mixed schooling, but the town had resented that break with tradition. The rape of a student by a classmate had the town bristling. To the conservative Sunni community, the regime was bent on "alienating" the believers from their culture and religion. There was no shortage of grievances: the government had fired schoolteachers for donning the head cover, and the lines were sharply drawn here, when this khatib came forth with his sermon.

The security forces were quick to notice Shaykh Anas. He was asked to provide a tape of his sermon—by decree, all Friday sermons are taped and made available upon request. He supplied the tape but refused a request to go to the security headquarters. He was certain he would be arrested. The head of local security called on him. The shaykh defended himself. He noted that he was fulfilling his religious obligation, commanding right, forbidding evil, and calling for reform. There was nothing seditious, he said, in what he had done. Word spread of Shaykh Anas's troubles, and people from neighboring Sunni villages came to Baniyas to pray in his mosque. This was early in the rebellion, and the security forces pulled back. Their restraint had not been cast aside. There was no deep political education in the town, Shaykh Anas observed. The chant was "Freedom"—this was the vocabulary the crowd knew.

The regime dispatched a high-ranking religious functionary to deal with Shaykh Anas—the mufti of Tartus. The young cleric was told to stick to religious matters and avoid political subjects. He was not awed by the rank of the visitor. The Sunni religious institution was a handmaiden of the regime, and Shaykh Anas stood his ground. The security services and the religious institution were twins, Shaykh Anas said to me. The ministry of religious endowments was worse than the secular organs of the state: the minister was a true cynic who didn't bother hiding his subservience to the ruler and his love of official perks and favors. The religious institution had bartered its soul and sense of mission for official favors. A day before our meeting, Shaykh Ahmad Sadiq, an ambitious cleric in Damascus and the prayer leader of Anas bin Malik Mosque, had been assassinated. He was several years younger than Shaykh Anas and had had a meteoric rise, including a mosque in the capital and financial remuneration from the regime. Shaykh Anas spoke of him without glee. That man had drawn close to the mukhabarat, he was not a learned man of the religious guild, he drew very few people to his mosque, and his sermons were an abysmal failure, Shaykh Anas said. The accommodation with the regime was the choice of a failed man, Shaykh Anas said.

Shaykh Anas had done what he could for Baniyas. But the regime was on his trail. He was smuggled out of the country, and then his wife and four children followed him to Turkey. His first stop was the refugee camps in Antakya, by the border with Syria. But the Turkish authorities sensed trouble, and the Damascus regime had sympathizers and agents among the refugees. He was advised to go to Istanbul. Exile was hard, he was trying to learn the Turkish language, and he worried about his children now attending a Sudanese school. He communicates on Skype with his followers back home. He was a man of the coast, and for all the dreadfulness of the regime, he held out hope for his homeland. He did not think that there would be massive retribution among the Alawis. He knew the coast, he said, and after the turmoil would come reconciliation. The country was being severed from its heritage, and he believed this rebellion was destined to give it a new lease on life.

KHALED KHOJA was at the heart of the work of the Syrian National Council in Turkey. He was a physician and an entrepreneur in health care, and the rebellion found him in its hour of need. He was a dual national, fluent in Turkish, and knew his way through Ankara and Istanbul. Born in 1965, he had come to

Turkey as a young man, after spending two years in prison. He had been sent to prison at age 15, along with his mother. They both were punished for his father's political activism. The father was active in the physicians' syndicate, a sympathizer of the Muslim Brotherhood. The father was to suffer a prison sentence of thirteen years. In Khaled's case, his imprisonment came in two periods. He was released on the condition of informing on his peers, or "writing reports" as the regime language had it. He had not complied and was picked up again. He did not think he was the youngest of the political prisoners, as the sins of the fathers were visited on the sons in the Baathist dictatorship.

In prison, he found his faith in Islam. It gave him solace and enabled him to endure the solitude and the cruelty. There was one thing worse than torture, he said. It was hearing others being tortured. He recalled one baron of the security apparatus, Mohamed Nassif. Nassif was one of the closest aides of Hafez al-Assad, and he was still at the nerve center of the intelligence services as this new rebellion raged. There was something odd about Nassif, Khaled recalls. He was given to visiting the political prisoners and engaging them in what passed for a friendly dialogue. Nassif, an Alawite, taunted the Islamists: they believed in heaven and hell, while he, on the other hand, was an agnostic who enjoyed the things of the world. Heaven, Nassif said, was his world—a warm abode, power, women, good food, and a life of ease. Hell was the world that these prisoners made for themselves. Young Khaled did not bend. He took to prayer, and kept the practice ever since. He described himself as a Muslim modernist, and the label was perfect for him: a stylish man, thin and well-dressed, a true cosmopolitan in his manners and bearing.

It was his grandfather who looked after him and enabled him to make the passage to Turkey. The extended family had had many Turks within its ranks. He recalls one incident that hooked him on the ways of Turkish democracy. Turkey's president, Turgut Ozal, had come to visit Khaled's school. He drove his own car, and the students mobbed him. One student had reached out and stuffed a note in Ozal's pocket. Ozal had asked what the boy had given him. The boy had said that the note would be self-explanatory. Ozal persisted, and the boy then whispered into the president's ear. Ozal, a bear of a man, gregarious and fond of banter, had then patted the boy on the head and told him that his request would be met. Khaled had once seen the forbidding Hafez al-Assad at a great remove. He was taking part in a May Day parade, and he and his schoolmates had marched in front of the despot. They had rifles assigned to them—but without ammunition. So great was the distance separating the dictator from the schoolboys, Khaled could not really claim that he had seen the ruler. This encounter in Turkey showed the ways of a more humane society.

Khaled was born in Damascus. I watched him with his fellow Syrians, and with the staff at the spare offices that housed the Syrian National Council. He regarded them with patience—and a measure of sympathy. His old country had fallen behind, and its people needed his skills. He was tireless. In the time I spent with him, which was well over a week, I was not sure he spent much time with his wife and children. He was in a state of permanent exhaustion. He was the most worldly of the people around him. His English was excellent, and he followed the American pronouncements on Syria with keen curiosity. He was puzzled by the passivity of American power. He was waiting for deliverance. He had about him, though, an attitude of guarded optimism. The regime was destined to fall, he believed. He was less certain of the timing and the costs. He did not need to retrieve his old world in Damascus; he had a bigger country that was his home now. But the obligation toward Syria was in his bloodstream, and so was a passion for the world of politics. Indeed, he had wanted to study political science, he told me. But his mother had drawn a line. She wanted for him medical school, a safe career, and a distance from all political matters. He had been the obedient son, and then the rebellion came knocking on his door. He spoke with affection of his aged father. The man had been timid at first, when the rebellion broke out. It was hard to persuade him to take part in the demonstrations in front of the Syrian consulate in Istanbul. But courage had come to him, and he was to tell his son, with no small measure of pride, that he taken part in a demonstration in Dubai.

The young physician was resigned to his course: there would be no normalcy for him until this rebellion had upended the dictatorship. His business and his family life no longer held him.

IT WAS KHALED KHOJA who suggested that I spend some time with "Abu Hazem," or Riad Shaqfa, the secretary-general of the Muslim Brotherhood. We met in the offices of the Syrian National Council, and Shaqfa came with his son, a polite and quiet young man. I recognized in Shaqfa right away the style and mannerisms of the "new" Muslim Brotherhood. He had a trim beard, a sweater under his jacket, and an air of reserve and accessibility. He was born in Hama in 1944, and the mark of that city, as I understood from him and his son, defined him and stayed with him in his years of exile. He was a civil engineer—engineering, of all professional choices, recurs in the ranks of the Islamists. He had fled Syria in 1980, during the war between the

Brotherhood and the regime. He was keenly aware of the burden of the long exile, and he spoke of Syria's realities with modesty. He was not anticipating a political kingdom if and when the regime falls. The rulers had changed the country, he admitted. They worked their will on it and corrupted its political and religious life. The House of Assad has ruled for four decades, he said, and it will take more than four decades to repair and heal the country.

The years in exile had not been easy. He had made his way to Iraq and lived in Baghdad until 2006. The Syrian regime, known for striking down its critics in foreign lands, had dispatched one of its killers to Iraq. He had shot Shaqfa in the leg, and the recovery was not easy. He told me he had forgiven his would-be assassin, a gun for hire that the security services recruited and then disposed of. After Iraq, he had made his way to northern Lebanon, to Tripoli, a conservative Sunni town with strong ties to the Brotherhood. In Tripoli, being born in Hama was considered a blessing, and he knew the saving grace of genuine sympathy.

Shaqfa spoke of Syria's past with pride. He narrated it without excessive zeal, almost as a man giving a civics lesson. In his reckoning, Syria was a country of religious pluralism. He harked back to the interwar years when Christians had a prominent role in Syrian politics. He acknowledged that it would not be easy to restore harmony among the sects. He was a "son of Hama," he said, and he knew that the past was not a time of bliss. There had been feuds between Hama and its Alawi hinterland, but these were feuds born of ignorance, of urban pride in the face of peasantry. Now it is the Alawis who will have to adjust to this new Syria. He did not believe that the sins of the rulers and their enforcers should become collective Alawi sins. He spoke of the regime's skills as one describes the ways of evil genius. He was not alone in the way he marveled at the cunning of Hafez al-Assad. He beheld the ways of his own community—the Sunni majority—with some puzzlement. They had submitted to the rule of the few and bent to the will of a dictator, and now in rebellion they could see for themselves that they had forged their own chains. The rulers, he said, had an eye for the weakness of those they sought to corrupt: they gave them what they yearned for—money, power, the company of women. Thus they were able to take the majority out of political life and reduce them to spectators to their own destiny. But all had been altered now, he said. The Syrian people will not return to the obedience and passivity of the past. The performance of the Syrian opposition had not been perfect, but the sacrifices of the Syrian people overwhelmed these concerns. He would not rebuke Damascus and Aleppo for their relative quiescence; he knew the weight and the burden of official terror.

He circled the matter of the Brotherhood's attitude toward the religious minorities. The regime, he said, had poisoned the well. It shelters behind the minority communities while claiming to be their protector. The Muslim Brotherhood had always reached out to the minorities. He looked to Egypt, the birthplace of the Brotherhood. In Egypt, in the time of the Brotherhood founder, Hassan al-Banna, Copts were at peace with the Brotherhood. They worked in its offices, and they ran on its parliamentary lists. The same was true in Syria before radical soldiers and ideologues disfigured political life. Shaqfa had a special reverence for a political figure from the Syrian past, a Protestant lawyer and politician by the name of Faris al-Khoury. Khoury had been a speaker of parliament and a minister; he had had a long political run. He had been prime minister three times, the last time as late as 1954, when he must have been in his late seventies. He had been an able leader and Syria, Shaqfa says, never quibbled about his religious faith.

He spoke of the Western powers as a man resigned to their practices. The United States, France, and Britain had not been true to their own principles. They had given aid and comfort to the Arab tyrannies. In doing so, they betrayed their own principles and made it easier for the dictatorships. He gave me the standard statement that he did not want to see Western military intervention in his country, but the drift of a long conversation and his keen sense of the region's politics suggested otherwise. He read Iran's commitment to the regime, and that of Hezbollah, with precision and realism. They were in this fight to the finish, he said, and there would be no reconciliation with them. Hezbollah prided itself on being a "resistance movement" that abhors repression, and there it was standing with the tyrant against his victim.

The new Syria would not be ruled by the Brotherhood, he said. It was banned by the regime in 1980, and membership was punishable by death. The Brotherhood had grown old, he said. He pointed to his son sitting by his side, and said that this young man, born in Iraq, would be subject to prosecution in Syria on grounds of his parentage. It had been a scorched-earth policy against the Brotherhood, and it had debilitated the movement. Men were sent to their death on the mere whiff of suspicion that they belonged to the Brotherhood. Judges would condemn them even if they denied affiliation with the Brotherhood.

There was an Islamist wave in the region, and this gave him heart. The electoral victories of men like him in Tunisia and Egypt and the ascendency of Islamists in Turkey bode well for Syria. Turkey was close to Syria, geographically and culturally, and the economic and political performance of Turkey under the Justice and Development Party of Prime Minister Erdogan was a powerful rebuttal, he observed, to all those who had insisted that political Islam foretold failure and ruin. His own utopia, Shaqfa said, was a "civic state" in which all Syrians had access to the dignity and decency of a normal life.

Memories of Hama ran through his reflections. He knew its reputation for religious intolerance, and brushed it aside. There was a Christian politician in Hama, he recalled. Elie Nusur was an ally of the Brotherhood, and he ran for parliament on the Brotherhood slate. His own father, he said, had been a close friend of the bishop of Hama. The two men visited each other on religious occasions. The city of his birth in the Syrian interior was not idyllic. He knew that, and he saw that bloody past through the prism of experience and exile. Hama had been made to suffer for its religious devotion. He had no interest in revisiting the past. He had no home in Hama. The regime had confiscated the property of those who had risen against it. But he was in Turkey now, his Iraqi-born son by his side, and he was confident that the city of his youth would have room for them both.

FROM AFAR, powers keen to keep their distance from Syria spoke of the "opaqueness" of the Syrian opposition. This was a reprise of what had been said of the Libyans when they rose against their dictator. But there was nothing opaque about the opposition leaders I met. Ambassador Bassam Imadi epitomized all that was familiar about the Syrian bourgeoisie. He was a Damascene who had risen to the upper rungs of the diplomatic service. His English was polished and precise. He was a gregarious, confident man with no eagerness to please. He had defected only months earlier and made his way to Istanbul. He had been ambassador to

Sweden and had wearied of representing so sullied a regime. Born
in 1950, Imadi had talent that had seen him through. The regime
gave ambassadorships mainly to its Alawi functionaries. Room
was made for him, and he spoke his mind as freely as the regime
would tolerate. His diplomatic career alternated assignments
abroad with stints of time at home. These frequent periods
abroad opened his eyes to the steady deterioration of his country.
The public institutions were coming apart, the educational system
was in shambles, and bribery and corruption had become a way
of life. It was no better in the diplomatic service; the embassies
were espionage centers in their own right. He did not want to
inform on Syrians abroad. He had weighed his options, and
defection to Turkey was his way out. He was a restless man, and
life in an Istanbul hotel was not what he would have willed for
himself.

A shrewd man, he knew the ways of the regime and its masters. He had had access to the councils of power. He had been in
enough meetings with Bashar al-Assad to see the inadequacies of
the ruler, the sycophancy that surrounded him, and the arrogance
the sycophancy bred in him. Behind the bluster of the regime,
Bassam Imadi sensed the cowardice of the ruling cabal. Sure
enough, the military commanders and intelligence barons were
cruel facing ordinary civilians. But he was certain they would
make a run for it should a serious blow come from the outside. It
was not just that cowardice that made an impression on him.
There was that deep sense of Alawite inadequacy in dealing with
Damascus and Damascenes. These Alawis in the inner circle of
power were keen to mimic the ways of the Damascenes, to marry
into them and draw on their skills. One anecdote amused him. A
high Alawi official had hired one of his distant relatives as a
driver, and the man had nearly wrecked the new car that this

official favored. The official then turned back to his old Damascene driver. It was like this in ways big and small. The Alawis had not used the time in power well.

Bassam Imadi was no fan of Old Man Assad, but he gave him his due: the dictator had been precise and methodical, loyal to a fault to those who stood by him. He recounted one episode that was symptomatic of the way the Old Man had worked his will on those around him. He had selected someone for a key intelligence portfolio. He gave him one of those dreaded intelligence files to review. The file was a detailed record, it turned out, of the intelligence officer himself. It was a thorough accounting of the man's financial dealings and sexual escapades and of his family's doings. The man was stunned, pledged fidelity to the ruler, and went on to assume the post had been given. Imadi had seen Hafez al-Assad at work: the discipline supplied by him had been lost, and the republic had become warring personal fiefdoms. Even the barons and warlords knew the system's defects, and they were unlikely to defend it to the end.

In a couple of days, Imadi was set to go to Tunis for a meeting of the Friends of Syria—a gathering of Western and Arab governments and international organizations looking for a way out of the country's ordeal. A worldly man schooled in diplomatic matters, he was not optimistic about that endeavor. He worried that the powers that be were leaving the Syrian people to the mercy of the regime. But he would go nonetheless. He had not given up career and home to idle his time away in Istanbul. The breakfast buffet in his hotel was not what he had bargained for. Away from home, the hotel life oppressed him and the restlessness burst through his courtly manners. He had bet on this rebellion and yearned for a functioning, modern state he would not be ashamed to serve.

Samir Nashar, a spokesman of the Syrian National Council, was a man of Aleppo. The businessman of means was 67 years of age, elegant, and well-groomed. There was in him the practicality and good sense of his native city. Over a meal by the Bosphorus, he contemplated Syria's malady against the background of Istanbul's order and prosperity. The weather had broken, a cold wave had yielded, and Istanbul was brilliant in the sun. He remembered Turkey in leaner times and his Turkish friends on this side of the border who would ask him to bring them coffee, razors, and little gadgets from Syria. Now Syria had become a backwater, a land of utter failure, and Turkey prosperous and at peace. There was no ideology in Nashar. He was, by my reckoning, a secularist to the core. He belonged to a generation that had given itself over to Arab nationalism only to be betrayed and to witness the rise of a regime of plunder and cruelty. He had a knack for the media—he was a well-spoken man of good looks and poise—and the meal was interrupted by a request for an interview from Al Jazeera. If he doubted the prospects of the rebellion, Nashar didn't let it show. There would be a huge task for him were the regime to falter. He was a believer in property and free markets. He didn't worry about the Islamists inheriting the new order. The Turkish way fortified him in his belief that the Syrians were a practical lot who would restore their country if given a chance. The Syrian National Council had a leader, the Paris-based academic Burhan Ghalioun. The leader, who had scholarly treatises to his name and a preference for the public sector, was an intellectual in the French tradition. Nashar didn't worry about him. There was enough room in Syria for Ghalioun, and for the time-honored skills of a savvy son of Aleppo.

CHAPTER ELEVEN

Fragments of a Past
Mourned and Dreaded

I N *DAMASCUS BETWEEN DEMOCRACY AND DICTATOR-*
SHIP, a book by Syrian author Sami Moubayed and published in 2000, I came across a black-and-white photograph
from 1955. Two Syrian leaders of that era, elegant men in formal
attire, are shaking hands. One of them has the sash of the presidency: the outgoing president, Hashem al-Atasi. Before the parliament, he is handing the reins of office to his successor, Shukri
al-Quwwatli. Both men hailed from the same social and political
milieu: the urban elite, landholders, and men of means. Both were
schooled in Istanbul, in the administrative academies of the
Ottoman bureaucracy, and raised in a tradition of public service.
Quwwatli was twenty years younger. He had been president
before, between 1943 and 1949. More to the point, he was a
nationalist hero who had been exiled by the French and had come
back to secure their departure from Syria by 1946. It was a peaceful transition of power, and three years later Quwwatli would
relinquish the presidency and make room for a doomed union
with Egypt—the United Arab Republic—as a Gamal Abdel
Nasser craze gripped Syria.

There was no presidency-for-life then, no robotic, unthinking
crowds chanting "Assad forever"—*Al-Assad ila al-abadd*. There
were no statues of Quwwatli or Atasi in every town square. It is

not likely that the demeaning cry of "with our souls and our blood we sacrifice ourselves for you" to the leader of the moment had been heard in that era. Quwwatli was a dominant figure, but it never occurred to him that the presidency would be bequeathed to a son of his, like a family heirloom. That political order was not perfect, and coup makers disrupted it repeatedly, the first time in 1949, a handful of years after independence. And then the military men would put its feebleness on display in 1963, when they pushed it into its grave. Syrians of a certain age remember that history, all the more treasured and adorned against the background of the drab tyranny that got hold of them in the years to come. Younger Syrians do not possess that history, but it was there for them, narrated by their elders. Their wrath at their current condition must on some level be nourished by the knowledge that they were not, by some genetic code, fated for despotism.

In the midst of this grief, Amal Hanano, a reporter for *Jadaliyya*, an interesting new online publication, came forth with a new appreciation of Quwwatli. She located and profiled at length a daughter of that historic leader. The daughter, Hana, now a woman in her seventies, was living in exile in Paris. She had been in France for decades and before that Lebanon. But in the way of exiles, she had carried with her a memory of Damascus and a storied family history of "eight hundred years" in that city. Memory retouched and adorned that past. "I was born in Damascus. When I first opened my eyes, I opened them in Damascus. Damascus taught us how to welcome and open our hearts to everyone."

Sitting under a large portrait of her father, a man with a red fez and a suit in the dignified late Ottoman style, she remembered a man of rectitude, his life a mirror of Syria's destiny. Fittingly for the aura and the myth, he had died in 1967 in Beirut, in the immediate aftermath of the Six-Day War and the loss of the Golan Heights. For a man who had been the "father" of his country and the seminal figure of its struggle for independence, the incumbent president at the time, a radical Baathist named Nur al-Din al-Atasi, had not wanted to grant his family permission to bury him in Damascus. Only the intercession of the Saudi monarch, King Faisal, had secured that permission. The Syrian people had not forgotten him, the daughter proudly recalls. "The road to Damascus was lined with thousands of people on both sides with their hands open, reciting the Quran and weeping for their leader." The government had wanted no public display of sorrow for the man, but the Damascenes would pay the authorities no heed. "At the Hijaz station, the people broke through the door of the ambulance and pulled out the coffin." The corpse of the deceased "glided over a sea of hands, dancing as if in a wedding, floating on their fingertips." The mourners prayed for him three times in the Umayyad Mosque and twice more in other mosques. The regime had declared war on the "feudalism" and the "backwardness" of the past, but the mourners knew better. The deceased leader was buried in the Shaghur, the old neighborhood where he was born—a popular quarter which his family had never abandoned.

An exquisite little item appeared in the readers' comments about that president and his time. It was culled from *Al Jareeda Rasmieh* (The Official Gazette) in 1949. The House of Deputies had rejected a request from the president of the republic to buy a new official car. Instead, he was allowed 75 Syrian pounds for repairing the old car, "following the report of the mechanic." There had been no special privileges for members of his family. They were a people of some means, but the public treasury was off-limits to them. Quwwatli had high regard for the independent spirit and temperament of the population. To his successor, she recalls, he famously said: "I leave you with a population where everyone thinks they are a leader." Now Syria is "cursed," she said, its constitution shredded. "We fought the French, kicked them out, but we were honorable opponents, and they were foreign occupiers. Today we are fighting one of our own, who attacks the people and the children. That is what is horrifying."

She talked of a Damascus the young reporter had never seen. She had visited the city two years earlier, on April 17, Independence Day. She had walked through her old neighborhood, "now in ruins." She was startled to see that there were no celebrations for Independence Day. This was a Damascus she did not know. She had stayed in a hotel because her family has "nothing in Syria, no home, not even a well." She dreams of owning a small house in Old Damascus, "scented with the trace of Damascus, scented with the spring of Damascus. I miss the apricot blossoms and the sheep in the Ghouta." The Ghouta, the gardens and the orchards that once circled Damascus, had been claimed by urban sprawl, and she knew it. She follows the news of this rebellion on Facebook, and even Twitter. She has hopes for it, but fears that it could yet come to grief and be "stolen" from those who had conquered the fear. She had a special pedigree, but she was hardly unique in her yearning for a country that violence and dictatorship—and official plunder, demography, and urban sprawl—had altered beyond recognition. In a detail of the vanished Syrian past, Hana Quwwatli gave her interviewer a special gift: a picture of her father with the interviewer's grandfather, Ibrahim Hanano. They had been men of the same social stratum, one of them a figure of Damascus, the other a leader in Aleppo.

A second fragment comes courtesy of one of the country's preeminent writers in his autobiographical novel, *Fragments of*

Memory, published in 1975. The novelist Hanna Mina was born in 1924 in the city of Latakia, by the Mediterranean. He was a child of crushing poverty. His family would leave Latakia for the province of Alexandretta, which they would quit when the province was lost to Turkey in 1939. Mina had been able to secure only primary schooling. He was a self-taught man who had worked on the docks and as a hairdresser before making his way to Damascus for a career in writing and journalism. Damascus was good to him, but he always yearned for Latakia and the sea. He wished that Damascus would move toward the sea, or that the sea would reach it. Mina never adorned or embellished. In his hands the misery of the Syrian poor, his family included, is rendered with heartbreaking honesty. His astonishing output, well over thirty works of fiction, is a record of the life of Syria in our time. He was in and out of prison nine times—under the French in the first decade of independence, and during the brief union between Syria and Egypt. He had known a decade of exile in China and Europe. Imprisoned during the Nasserite interlude, he had wept and grieved over the death of Nasser in 1970.

A memory comes to him, perhaps from the late 1940s. By then he had lost his older sisters to disease and toil. He is with his mother in one of the wealthier quarters of Beirut when they encounter an "old *fellah* from the Latakia countryside giving up his young daughter as a servant in one of those houses. He was on the point of leaving her as she clung to him in tears and pleads with him, 'I don't want to stay here, I don't want . . . Take me with you; I'm kissing your hand. Take me, Father, take me with you.'" The writer's mother is shaken by the scene. It was a scene from her own past. "I don't know the fellah or his daughter, but that sight saddened me. Your oldest sister cried like that when I left her as a child to work in the village headman's house. She clung to my dress like this child to her father's trousers. She too pleaded, 'I don't want to stay here. Take me with you Mother. I'm kissing your hand. Take me with you.'"

The Latakia countryside was Alawi country, and the fellah giving up his daughter for what was, for all intents and purposes, indentured servitude was an Alawi peasant. In my boyhood in Beirut, there were countless Alawi servants, young girls delivered into families with means to feed the girls' families back home. There was, and remains, distress in Syria beyond the ones inflicted by political life. There were the injustices of birth and station, the chasm that separated—as Arabs would put it—the children of the lady from the children of the servant. A political life filled with conspiracy and violence—and some measure of yearning for justice—brought the Alawis to power, and the gun and the uniform had granted them a measure of retribution against those who had it easier and better in life. They were in no mood to go back to the servitude; the pendulum had not stopped in the middle.

M Y NARRATIVE ENDS, but the regime still stands. The suffering of the Syrian people has not drawn to a close. It is not pretty in Libya: the militias fight over the country's direction, even though the sordid chapter of the Muammar el-Qaddafi tyranny has closed. Egyptians may not think the brilliant revolution in Tahrir Square, those magical 18 days that toppled Hosni Mubarak, fulfilled all their hopes, but the despised pharaoh is gone. Tunisians do not dwell on the dictator that they overthrew as his exile in Saudi Arabia consigns his petty kleptocracy to memory.

In the same vein, Ali Abdullah Saleh, the acrobat who ruled Yemen for three decades, if that word applies to the anarchy of that sad land, stepped aside and left the country to its sorrows. Social peace has not come to Bahrain, yet the protesters there have not sought to overthrow the monarchy and the violence remains relatively restrained. Of the Arab societies stirred by the turmoil of 2010–2011, Syria stands alone in the price paid by its peoples, and in the cruelty and tenacity of the regime.

To state the obvious, I did not hide my sympathies in this book. No author is a moral umpire calling strikes, and I did not pretend to be one in this endeavor. I never doubted the ability of the Syrian people to create a more humane order than this dreaded regime. Not for me were the worries about the "opaqueness" of the opposition, or the prospect of Syria turning into an Islamist dystopia. The Syrian people have known hell, and I am certain that whatever order they arrive at will honor the sacrifices they have made.

Regimes can hold on even after they have been emptied of all moral legitimacy.

The dictator who paid Homs a lightning visit after he inflicted on it bottomless suffering expressed his moral emptiness. He had come to taunt the bereaved city. To my knowledge, his father did not make that kind of visit to Hama three decades earlier, so soon after the slaughter.

There is no denying that the powers-that-be in the order of states let down the Syrian people. As of this writing, speculation mounts that the scale of the brutality will force the powers to ride to the rescue. The precedents of Bosnia and Kosovo have been invoked, and the cavalry shamed into intervention. One thing is certain, the people of Syria have shown their determination in the face of merciless terror. The bonds between them and their rulers have been severed. Amid the suffering, Syrians stubbornly recall a better country. May they know the grace of the normalcy that has eluded them for so long.

April 2012

CHAPTER ONE: *Prologue: The Inheritor*

Ibn Khaldun's *The Muqaddimah: An Introduction to History*, translated from the Arabic by Franz Rosenthal, Princeton, New Jersey, Princeton University Press, 1969, paints an eloquent portrait of the inevitable deterioration of a ruling family.

Dissident Burhan Ghalioun recalls the enthusiasm for the earlier Damascus Spring. See Sharif Abdel Kouddous "A Lifetime of Resistance in Syria," *The Nation*, September 2011, and Amal Hanano, "Portraits of a People," *Jadaliyya*, October 31, 2011.

CHAPTER TWO: *Come the Mountain People*

For background on jihadists, see political journalist Nibras Kazimi's Hoover study of 2010, *Syria through Jihadist Eyes: A Perfect Enemy*, Stanford, California, Hoover Institution Press.

For a thorough study of the heterodox Shia cults, see Matti Moosa's *Extreme Shiites: The Ghulat Sects*, Syracuse, New York, Syracuse University Press, 1987.

The mid-nineteenth-century author W.M. Thomson in his remarkable book, *The Land and The Book*, London, T. Nelson & Sons, 1872, spent 30 years in Syria and Palestine as a missionary.

The autonomy and the benefits that the French gave the Alawis can be seen in Albert Hourani's *Syria and Lebanon: A Political Essay*, London Oxford University Press, 1946, p. 51.

Itamar Rabinovich, in his book, *The View from Damascus*, Portland, Oregon, Vallentine Mitchell, 2008, brings order to the tangled history of the Alawis, French, Druze, Kurds, and Sunnis.

The Alawite petition of 1936 can be found in Matti Moosa's *Extreme Shiites: The Ghulat Sects*, Syracuse, New York, Syracuse University Press, 1987, and Philip Khoury's *Syria Under the French Mandate*, Princeton, New Jersey, Princeton University Press, 1987, tells the tale of Sulayman al-Murshid.

For more on the mufti of Jerusalem, see Gitta Yaffe-Schatzmann's "Alawi Separatists and Unionists: The Events of 25 February, 1936," *Middle Eastern Studies*, Volume 31, Number 1, January 1995.

Martin Kramer, in "Syria's Alawis and Shi'ism," in Martin Kramer, editor, *Shi'ism, Resistance and Revolution*, Westview Press, Boulder, Colorado, 1987, pp. 237–254, explains the rupture between the Alawis and the Sunnis.

CHAPTER THREE: *The Time of the Founder*

In his seminal book, *Syria's Peasantry, the Descendants of Its Lesser Rural Notables, and Their Politics*, Princeton, New Jersey, Princeton University Press, 1999, Hanna Batatu captures Hafez al-Assad's rise to power and his purging of friends and foes alike.

In a moving memoir, *The Betrayals of Language and Silence*, Beirut, 2006, Ahmad Faraj Birqdar tells us of the heartbreaking visits from his daughter and the poetry they share. Birqdar's court testimony appears as an annex to his memoir.

In Farbrice Balanche's "Alaouites: Une Secte au Pouvoir," *Outre Terre* 2, 12, 2006, pp. 73–96, he eloquently illustrates the finesse with which the elder Assad dealt with the issue of Alawi religion and its credibility.

To understand Hafez al-Assad's ties with the Syrian peasantry, see Hanna Batatu's *Syria's Peasantry, the Descendants of Its Lesser rural Notables, and Their Politics*, Princeton, New Jersey, Princeton University Press, 1999.

The rebellion in Aleppo in 1979 is depicted in a novel by Khaled Khalifa, a son of Aleppo and a brilliant novelist. Khalifa, who was born in 1964, was in his late teens during the barbarous time that was to have its spellbinding chronicle in his 2008 novel, *Madih al-Karahiya* (In Praise of Hatred), translated into French, *Eloge de la Haine*.

Michel Seurat, in *L'Etat de Barbarie*, Paris, Editions Du Seuil, 1989, captures the insurgency in Aleppo, the ruthless response of Hafez Assad's brother Rifaat, commander of the Defense Battalions, and the attack and slaughter at Palmyra prison. Seurat, born in Tunisia in 1947, was an exacting researcher and writer. He had done original work in Syria and Lebanon, and his knowledge of Tripoli was second to none. He was kidnapped in Beirut by Islamic Jihad in 1985 and was to die in captivity at the age of 38. *L'Etat de Barbarie* was published posthumously. The essays in it on Syria stand out for their mix of genuine scholarship and a flair for writing.

For the social history of Syria, see the Lebanese journalist Jihad Al-Zeine's article, "The Sectarian Riddle in the Democratic Transformation of Syria," *An-Nahar*, July 29, 2011.

CHAPTER FOUR: *False Dawn*

For a personal insight into Lebanon's struggles against Syrian maneuvering, see George P. Shultz's *Turmoil and Triumph: Diplomacy, Power, and the Victory of the American Ideal*, New York, Simon and Schuster, 1993, p. 206.

For a thorough account of the transition from Assad Sr. to Bashar, see Eyal Zisser's *Commanding Syria, Bashar al-Asad and the First Years in Power*, London, I. B. Tauris Academic Press, 2006.

The minutes of the meeting between Rafik Hariri, Bashar al-Assad, and their deliberations were leaked. The Lebanese newspaper *Al Joumhouria* would print the full text on August 4, 2011.

Anthony Shadid in "Beirut Blast Kills Foe of Syria," *The Washington Post*, December 13, 2005, writes about the assassination of Lebanese journalist Gebran Tueni.

I found several useful insights from mining dispatches released by Wiki-Leaks. One on Gebran Tueni is from the U.S. Embassy in Damascus Dispatch "The Killing of Gebran Tueni," December 19, 2005.

For the Bush administration's Diplomacy of Freedom and the Cedar Revolution, see George W. Bush's *Decision Points*, New York, Crown Publishers, 2010, p. 412.

The Iraq Study Group Report: The Way Forward, James A. Baker III and Lee H. Hamilton, co-chairs, New York, Vintage Books, 2006, explains the impetus for re-engagement with Syria and Iran as the popularity for the Iraq war wanes.

Syrian Intelligence Chief Attends Ct dialogue with S/Ct Benjamin, U.S. Embassy in Damascus, February 24, 2010.

Senator John Kerry's explanation of his view on Syria can be seen in his Letter to the Editor, *The Wall Street Journal*, June 17, 2011.

Human Rights Watch has been a valuable source of information throughout this conflict, *A Wasted Decade: Human Rights in Syria During Bashar al-Assad's First Ten Years in Power*, New York, 2010.

CHAPTER FIVE: *The Boys of Deraa*

Jay Solomon and Bill Spindle, in their piece in *The Wall Street Journal*, "Syria Strongman: Time for 'Reform,'" January 31, 2011, give the reader an illuminating interview with Bashar Al-Assad.

The International Crisis Group reports have provided a clear reading of the rebellion. See International Crisis Group, Popular Protest in North Africa and the Middle East (VI): The Syrian People's Slow-Motion Revolution, July 2011, Report Number 108.

The protests in Baniyas are depicted in Mohamad Abisamra's "From the Diary of the Syrian Intifada," *An-Nahar*, October 9, 2011.

CHAPTER SIX: *The Phantoms of Hama*

British traveler and writer Robin Fedden's writings on Hama are of particular interest. See Robin Fedden, *Syria: An Historical Appreciation*, London, Robert Hale Limited, 1946.

Fabrice Balanche's *La Region Alaouite et Le Pouvoir Syrien*, Editions Karthala, Paris, 2006, and his essay "Geographie de la Revolte Syrienne," published in La Revue *Outre Terre*, n29 d'octobre-décembre 2011, infuse geography and sociology and provide a unique understanding of Syria, its communities, and its territories.

For a country closed to the outside, Facebook, Twitter, and YouTube have been employed to send messages to the world. See Thomas Pierret's "The Syrian Exile Ulama Try to Answer the Devout Bourgeoisie Via YouTube," *Mediapart*, October 21, 2011.

One of the few journalists allowed access to Damascus, and a meeting with businessman and Bashar al-Assad's maternal cousin Rami Makhlouf, was *New York Times* journalist Anthony Shadid. See his "Syrian Elite to Fight Protests to the End," *The New York Times*, May 10, 2011.

Turkish Prime Minister Erdogan's remarks on Syria were made in *An-Nahar*, November 2, 2011.

The great risks taken by army defectors is illustrated in the story of Lt. Col. Hussein Harmoush; Ivan Watson, "The Mysterious Disappearance of Hussein Harmoush," CNN, October 14, 2011.

Nibras Kazimi is a young scholar who knows Iraq and Syria. See "The Syrian Scene and Its Impact on Iraq," *Imara wa Tijarah*, April 19, 2011.

Charles Glass, in his book *Tribes With Flags: A Dangerous Passage Through the Chaos of the Middle East*, New York, The Atlantic Monthly Press, 1990, takes his reader from Alexandretta to Aqaba with a visit to Hama a few years after the massacres there.

CHAPTER SEVEN: *The Truth of the Sects*

Lebanese journalist Michael Young, in his piece "Lebanon's Troublesome Political Priest," *The Daily Star*, September 15, 2011, in unsparing words questions the Maronite patriarch's support for the Syrian rulers.

Michel Kilo, "A Plea to the Maronite Patriarch," *Al Arabiya*, September 19, 2011, brings weight to this argument regarding support by the Maronite Church for the regime in Syria. Kilo, in his 70s now, is a former inmate in Assad's prisons, a Christian, and a leading oppositionist.

Freya Stark (1893–1993) was an explorer and an amazingly prolific travel writer. Edward Atiyah in his book, *An Arab Tells His Story: A Study of Loyalties*, explains the fault lines between sect and community on Greater Syria. The passages from Edward Atiyah and Freya Stark can be found in Daniel Pipes's *Greater Syria*, New York, Oxford University Press, 1990.

For Lebanese Prime Minister Najib Mikati's story, see Radwan Aqeel, *An-Nahar*, August 7, 2011, "Report From Tripoli."

French academician Thomas Pierret has done exhaustive research in Syrian Islam and gives us a clear portrait in "Des Islamistes Syriens tend la main a la Communauté Alaouite," *Mediapart*, October 4, 2011.

A head of the "coalition of Syrian tribes," Ismael Khalidi spoke to *Al Watan Al Arabi*, September 30, 2011, in an interview by Sayyid Jubeil.

Syria through Jihadist Eyes: A Perfect Enemy, The Hoover Institution Press, 2010, Nibras Kazimi, through extensive research on the ground in Syria, supplies the reader with ample evidence of the coming unrest and uprising within Syria.

Controversial cleric Shaykh Ahmad Hassoun, a supporter of the Syrian regime, attracts animus from many quarters with his inflammatory remarks. U.S. Embassy Cables, WikiLeaks, dispatch of February 3, 2010, from the U.S. Embassy in Damascus, "Grand Mufti's Comments on Prophet Spark Rare Public Attacks." Nir Rosen, "A Conversation With Grand Mufti Hassoun," *Al Jazeera*, October 3, 2011. Mufti Hassoun's message for the Syrian people can be found in *Elaph*, October 9, 2011.

Joshua Landis, "Islamic Education in Syria: Undoing Secularism," *Insania*, Volume 13, September/December 2008, depicts the educational system in Syria under the Assads.

Anthony Shadid, "Syria's Sons of No One," *New York Times Magazine*, August 31, 2011, depicts the radicalism of the young men at the center of the Syrian rebellion.

CHAPTER EIGHT: *Sarajevo on the Orontes*

WikiLeaks disclosure on Homs and its Christian community's standing in that city. See "Outside the Capital: Local Leaders Discuss Challenges for Homs," U.S. Embassy in Damascus, February 3, 2010.

For insight into the composition of the Syrian army and its method of control, see Agence France-Presse, "Syrian Army Defectors Tell of Regime Ruthlessness," October 8, 2011.

Josh Wood, in his piece "Syrian Refugees in Lebanon Face Peril," *The New York Times*, October 19, 2011, depicts in stark terms the absence of protection offered Syrians seeking safety in Lebanon.

Shibli al-Aismay, an elderly Druze with no political agenda, was reportedly kidnapped while visiting his daughter. See Nada Bakri, "Syria Accused of Kidnapping in Lebanon," *The New York Times*, November 1, 2011.

Amnesty International has been vigilant in its reporting of the human tragedy in Syria. See *Health Crisis: Syrian Government Targets the Wounded and Health Workers*, 2011.

Andrew Gilligan interviewed Bashar al-Assad and toured the city of Hama during his trip to Syria in November 2011. In the city visit, the journalist met with the governor of the province. "Interview with Syria's President Assad," *The Sunday Telegraph*, October 30, 2011. Andrew Gilligan, "Inside Hama, The City of Fear and Ghosts," *The Daily Telegraph*, November 1, 2011.

CHAPTER NINE: *The Stalemate*

Amal Hanano, in her "Portrait of a People: Burhan Ghalioun," *Jadali-yya*, October 31, 2011, introduces her readers to this man in Paris, a professor and the head of the Syrian National Council.

Fadwa Soliman, an Alawite actress who broke with her sect and with her fear and showed up in Homs in November 2011 to offer her support for the protesters. Several days later, she was forced into hiding. See Basma Atasi's "Syria's Daring Actress," *Al Jazeera*, November 24, 2011. In March 2012, she turned up in Paris—she had fled the country through Jordan.

For Iraqi President Jalal Talabani's remarks on Western military intervention in Syria, see *Asharq Alawsat*, November 27, 2011.

The Report of the Independent International Commission of Inquiry on the Syrian Arab Republic, November 23, 2011, interviewed 223 victims and witnesses of alleged human rights violations, including civilians and defectors from the military and the security forces.

For a shrewd telling of the relationship between Syria and Iran, see Itamar Rabinovich's *The View From Damascus*, Portland, Oregon, Vallentine Mitchell, 2008.

Burhan Ghalioun gives his first interview as the new head of the Syrian National Council to Jay Solomon and Nour Malas, "Syria Would Cut Iran Military Tie, Opposition Head Says," *The Wall Street Journal*, December 2, 2011.

Michel Kilo, in his article "What Does the President Know?" *Asharq Alawsat*, December 14, 2011, raises the disturbing questions in many people's minds about the interview Bashar al-Assad gave to veteran journalist Barbara Walters on December 7, 2011.

As the Arab League monitors arrived in Damascus in December, there were two huge car bombs killing more than forty people. See Kareem Fahim's "Syria Blames Al Qaeda after Bombs Kill Dozens in Damascus," *The New York Times*, December 23, 2011.

A widely respected cleric in Syria, Karim al-Rajeh condemns Bashar al-Assad and his regime in *Asharq Alawsat*, December 25, 2011.

Patrick Seale was a biographer of Hafez al-Assad and is a leading political historian of modern Syria. His columns can be read online at his website, Patrickseale.com/Agence Global. See, in particular, "A Defiant Assad Sticks to His Guns," June 21, 2011.

See Josh Rogin, "The Obama Administration Secretly Preparing Options for Aiding the Syrian Opposition," *Foreign Policy*, posted December 28, 2011, and Mark Landlee, "A Wartime Leader Ends a War He Never Wanted," *The New York Times*, December 9, 2011.

Foreign intervention had been dismissed as being unpopular with the Syrians, but Samir Nashar, an executive board member of the Syrian National Council, offers a powerful rebuttal to that conventional view. See Ben Birnbaum, "Opposition Leader: Most Syrians Want Foreign Military Action," *The Washington Times*, January 2, 2012.

Tunisian President Moncef Marzouki's concerns about the violence in Syria are quoted in *An-Nahar*, January 12, 2012.

For Aleppo's Archbishop Jeanbart's remarks, see Agence France-Presse, January 11, 2012.

A young, courageous Shaykh Abdulijalil al-Said broke with Mufti Hassoun, and he is quoted in *Asharq Alawsat*, January 15, 2012.

Former Secretary of State Henry Kissinger has an unfailing eye for the ways of political leaders. His reflections on Hafez al-Assad are well worth a read. *Years of Upheaval*, Boston, Little, Brown & Company, 1982, p. 779.

Ali Asa'ad Watfa, "The Alawi Community in the Dock: A Sociological Reading," *Elaph*, January 5, 2012.

Arnold Toynbee, *A Study of History, Volume II*. The passage was quoted by the celebrated Lebanese philosopher and banker Michel Chiha, arguably the preeminent expositor of Lebanese nationalism. He quoted Toynbee in a 1953 lecture to al-Nadwa al-Lubnaniya, a prominent Beirut forum. Fifty years of that forum's lectures were collected and published by *Dar An-Nahar* in 1997.

CHAPTER ELEVEN: *Fragments of a Past Mourned and Dreaded*

Sami Moubayed, *Damascus Between Democracy and Dictatorship*, Lanham, Maryland, University Press of America, 2000. Amal Hanano, "A Syrian President's Daughter," *Jadaliyya*, December 6, 2011. The passages from Hanna Mina are from *Fragments of Memory, A Story of a Syrian Family*, University of Texas at Austin, 1993. (Translated by Olive Kenny and Lorne Kenny.)

ABOUT THE AUTHOR

FOUAD AJAMI is a senior fellow at the Hoover Institution and the co-chair of the Herbert and Jane Dwight Working Group on Islamism and the International Order. From 1980 to 2011 he was director of Middle East Studies at the Johns Hopkins University. He is the author of *The Arab Predicament, Beirut: City of Regrets, The Dream Palace of the Arabs*, and *The Foreigner's Gift*. His writings also include some four hundred essays on Arab and Islamic politics, U.S. foreign policy, and contemporary international history. Ajami has received numerous awards, including the Benjamin Franklin Award for public service (2011), the Eric Breindel Award for Excellence in Opinion Journalism (2011), the Bradley Prize (2006), the National Humanities Medal (2006), and MacArthur Fellows Award (1982). His research has charted the road to 9/11, the Iraq war, and the U.S. presence in the Arab-Islamic world.

HERBERT AND JANE DWIGHT

WORKING GROUP ON

ISLAMISM AND THE

INTERNATIONAL ORDER

The Herbert and Jane Dwight Working Group on Islamism and the International Order seeks to engage in the task of reversing Islamic radicalism through reforming and strengthening the legitimate role of the state across the entire Muslim world. Efforts will draw on the intellectual resources of an array of scholars and practitioners from within the United States and abroad, to foster the pursuit of modernity, human flourishing, and the rule of law and reason in Islamic lands— developments that are critical to the very order of the international system.

The Working Group is co-chaired by Hoover fellows Fouad Ajami and Charles Hill with an active participation by Director John Raisian. Current core membership includes Russell A. Berman, Abbas Milani, and Shelby Steele, with contributions from Zeyno Baran, Reuel Marc Gerecht, Ziad Haider, R. John Hughes, Nibras Kazimi, Bernard Lewis, Habib Malik, Camille Pecastaing, Lieutenant Colonel Joel Rayburn, and Joshua Teitelbaum.